Developing
Mathematical Thinking

D1194711

Developing Mathematical Thinking

A Guide to Rethinking the Mathematics Classroom

Jonathan D. Katz

ROWMAN & LITTLEFIELD
Lanham • Boulder • New York • Toronto • Plymouth, UK

Published by Rowman & Littlefield
4501 Forbes Boulevard, Suite 200, Lanham, Maryland 20706
www.rowman.com

10 Thornbury Road, Plymouth PL6 7PP, United Kingdom

British Library Cataloguing in Publication Information Available

Library of Congress Cataloging-in-Publication Data

Katz, Jonathan D., 1954– author.
  Developing mathematical thinking : a guide to rethinking the mathematics classroom / Jonathan D. Katz.
      pages cm
  Includes bibliographical references and index.
  ISBN 978-1-4758-1056-1 (cloth : alk. paper) — ISBN 978-1-4758-1057-8 (electronic) — ISBN 978-1-4758-1058-5 (electronic) 1. Mathematics—Study and teaching (Middle school) 2. Mathematics—Study and teaching (Secondary) 3. Inquiry-based learning. 4. Effective teaching. I. Title.
  QA11.2.K38 2014
  510.71'2—dc23

                                                                2014006877

Printed in the United States of America

Dear Reader,

This book has been written with great love and appreciation for mathematics and the desire to help teachers bring that emotion to their students. I would like to thank many colleagues and friends who have helped to make this book possible. They helped me in the early stages of this book and those who have been part of the new editions and ongoing editing as we all thought about what teachers are looking for in this point in time. They include Dr. Regine Philippeaux-Pierre, Marylin Cano, Mathew Sullivan, Toby Horowitz, Cassondra Zielinski, and Dr. Karen Lee. I want to express a special thank you to Joseph Walter, who has supported me in this work for the past ten years and was a central contributor to this book. Finally I would like to express my gratitude to Nathan Dilworth, who has helped in so many ways to make this book possible. He has been an editor, a thought partner, and a critical questioner.

I hope you find this book valuable to your work.
Sincerely,

Dr. Jonathan D. Katz

Contents

Preface

From a very early age I loved numbers. I was adding before I learned to read. Math made sense and there always seemed to be a right answer. How satisfying to a confused young boy trying to find his place in the world. Meanwhile, school did little to enhance my excitement about mathematics. I continued to do very well in mathematics class, but my passion for numbers and mathematical ideas seemed to wane. As I went to college, I moved away from mathematics and majored in physical education. I was ready to be a "gym" teacher when I went on an interview at a school and they asked if I would be willing to teach mathematics. I agreed to take this chance even though I felt unprepared. So my journey in mathematics education began at Walt Whitman Middle School in the Flatbush section of Brooklyn. I now had the chance to revisit a subject that gave me such excitement and joy at the age of three. I took many college mathematics courses and a whole new world was opened to me. I came to love mathematics once again.

I taught mathematics in New York City for twenty-four years to students as young as eleven and as old as nineteen. I have seen the struggle students have with understanding mathematical concepts and procedures and with solving problems. Students often complained about the uselessness of what they were learning. "Why do I need to know this?" is a mantra often heard in the mathematics classroom. Yet I have also seen the excitement on a student's face when an idea of mathematics begins to make sense.

In my first few years of teaching, I would have been classified as a conventional didactic teacher. I worked hard and had some success. But I always felt that I was fooling everybody. I was good at getting students to do well on standardized tests, but what were they really learning?

As the years went on, I incorporated new ideas into my teaching. Problem solving, art, and architecture became staples in my classroom. I loved creating learning experiences for my students where they thought about the patterns of mathematics and had to discover mathematical ideas, but I did it on a limited basis. I was viewed as a very successful teacher, but I still feared that I was a fake: good at getting students to do well on tests, but feeling that student understanding was all superficial. I would not have used the terms *procedural fluency* and *conceptual understanding*, but I felt I taught students ways to do mathematics, tricks of the trade, without real procedural fluency or deep conceptual understanding.

In my eighteenth year of teaching, I began to work in an alternative high school with students for whom English was a second language. This school was different than any school I had ever witnessed. It had a progressive philosophy toward education, including the belief in project-based instruction. In my early days at this school, I struggled with and questioned the school's philosophical beliefs. I did not understand how one would teach in this type of school. I had essentially seen teaching as the transmission of knowledge. That was the way I was taught and I never saw anyone do it differently. I wondered to myself, "What do they think teaching means?" I was scared and ready to run back to what I saw as comfortable. Meanwhile, I was amazed at what I saw all around me. Students seemed to like to learn at this school and the level of student engagement was very high. Over time I began to incorporate a new type of instruction into my classroom, inquiry-based instruction. I began to see my students' interest in mathematics grow as they were asked to discover mathematical concepts, apply their understandings in meaningful projects, and view mathematics as a creative experience. While students still struggled with understanding mathematical ideas, they began to appreciate the wonder, power, and beauty of mathematics.

In all my years of teaching, gnawing questions always went through my mind. Are my students really learning mathematics? What did the students get out of what they just learned? What was their experience in today's lesson? Why do they think I taught them what I did? Are they experiencing what I hoped they would experience?

When I left the classroom to become a mathematics coach, new experiences came into my life. I was now working with adults. Over these past nine years, my interest in inquiry-based instruction has grown enormously as I have worked with high-school mathematics teachers. I have supported teachers in thinking about how to get students to think about mathematical ideas in order to develop both conceptual understanding and procedural fluency. I have assisted teachers in creating inquiry experiences for their students through using interesting open-ended problems that would help students develop both strategic competence and adaptive reasoning. I have encouraged teachers to think about how to help students wonder about mathematics and appreciate its beauty with the goal of seeing that mathematics was worthwhile and even exciting. Meanwhile, I have also seen how teachers' beliefs and perceptions of mathematics and mathematics instruction have a great impact on how they teach. What does that mean in terms of student learning?

My journey in mathematics reached a new point when I decided to attend Teachers College as a doctoral student. I came to Teachers College wanting to make sense of my many years in mathematics, so full of unanswered questions but ready to learn new ideas so that I could be of use to other mathematics educators. I was able to complete a doctorate and write a dissertation that told the stories of teachers and students in four high-school mathematics classrooms. I tried to deepen our understanding of both conventional and inquiry-based instruction. It was my opening document that I hope shed some light on the debate in the mathematics world on how we should best instruct students in the mathematics classroom.

This book is the next step in my journey. It is a document that brings together my work as a teacher and a coach of teachers. It also is a document that honors the many authors, poets, philosophers, mathematicians, and educators who have affected my life over the years. They include Eli Siegel, Mario Salvadori, Paul Lockhart, Jo Boaler, Magdalene Lampert, Mark Driscoll, Walt Whitman, and Charles Dickens.

The reason I love teaching mathematics and feel passionate about it has always been and will always be the students and teachers. I have had the opportunity to work with thousands of students and hundreds of teachers over the past quarter century. I have thought about many of them as I worked on this book. They are still deeply a part of me.

I dedicate these lines of Walt Whitman to all the students I have had the privilege to teach, all the teachers I have worked and have had the chance to influence. You have all taught me so very much:

> *There was a child went forth everyday;*
> *And the first object he look'd upon that object he became*
> *And that object became a part of him for a day, or a certain part of the day,*
>   *or for many years, or stretching cycles of years.*

Introduction

Mathematics is a discipline filled with the beauty of interconnected ideas and patterns that continue to amaze and awe mathematical communities. Its uses are numerous and its influence substantial. Mathematics is a science and an art.

Teachers have a wonderful opportunity to help students appreciate this beauty and wonder. Polya (1945) once said:

> *Thus, a teacher of mathematics has a great opportunity. If he fills his allotted time with drilling his students in routine operations he kills their interest, hampers their intellectual development, and misuses his opportunity. But if he challenges the curiosity of his students by setting their problems proportionate to their knowledge, and helps them to solve their problems with stimulating questions, he may give them a taste for, and some means of, independent thinking.*

It is with great excitement that I present this book to all the school principals, mathematics teachers, and all other people interested in the transformation of the mathematics classroom to a place of excitement and imagination. This book, like all books, has a history. Work on it began in 2008 when math teachers and coaches gathered together to create a document that would help teachers think about how to use the ideas of inquiry in their everyday teaching. Today it has grown to become so much more. I see the book as a presentation of a way of teaching and learning mathematics. It is a book that can be used to move your students to a new place of thinking. It is a book that is both theoretical and immediately useful. Many people's ideas, including those of George Polya, are included in this book. These ideas come out of rigorous research and real classroom experiences. I am excited to share this book with you.

A little background is necessary as you read some of the documents in this book. The approach to teaching mathematics presented in this book is based on an inquiry approach. I have used two documents to help guide my thinking: the **Process Standards** from the National Council of Teachers of Mathematics *Principles and Standards for School Mathematics* (2000) and the **Five Strands of Mathematical Proficiency** from the National Research Council's report, *Adding It Up* (2001). They are documents that are very connected to each other yet are quite different. They are both very important in the development of a real mathematical thinker. The NCTM Process Standards are about the development of mathematical thinking through a problem-solving view of mathematics, while the Five Strands of Mathematical Proficiency reflect a more content-based approach, leading to conceptual and procedural understanding. They both have important things to say about the teaching and learning of mathematics and I believe the two documents combined give a more complete sense to the work I am encouraging teachers to do in their classrooms.

Recently the Common Core State Standards were introduced to the educators of the United States. The Standards for Mathematical Practice within the Common Core State Standards for Mathematics were based on the two documents that are central to the approach to mathematics teaching and learning presented in this book.

It is stated in the Common Core State Standards for Mathematics (CCSI, 2010):

> The Standards for Mathematical Practice describe varieties of expertise that mathematics educators at all levels should seek to develop in their students. These practices rest on important "processes and proficiencies" with long-standing importance in mathematics education. The first of these are the NCTM process standards of problem solving, reasoning and proof, communication, representation, and connections. The second are the strands of mathematical proficiency specified in the National Research Council's report *Adding It Up*: adaptive reasoning, strategic competence, conceptual understanding (comprehension of mathematical concepts, operations and relations), procedural fluency (skill in carrying out procedures flexibly, accurately, efficiently and appropriately), and productive disposition (habitual inclination to see mathematics as sensible, useful, and worthwhile, coupled with a belief in diligence and one's own efficacy).

While I respect the ideas presented within the Standards of Mathematical Practice, I have chosen to continue working with the NCTM process standards and the NRC strands of mathematical proficiency. I think they represent with great clarity two sets of standards for teaching and learning that will lead to both deep understanding of content and the ability to think mathematically.

While the two sets of standards are deeply connected and talk about common ideas, I view the NCTM Process Standards as five dimensions that are central to a student developing the ability to think mathematically and I view the NRC Five Strands of Mathematical Proficiency as the means to develop deep content knowledge through the interrelationship of conceptual understanding, procedural fluency strategic competence, and adaptive reasoning. Thus I use both sets of standards within my work and often integrate them. You will see throughout the book the use of these sets of standards, which I think will support the Common Core Standards of Mathematical Practice.

What Will You Find in This Book?

CHAPTER 1

- **A Vision of an Inquiry-based Mathematics Classroom**—This theoretical statement about an inquiry approach to teaching mathematics is based on the Five Strands of Mathematical Proficiency.
- **What Does an Inquiry Process Look Like in Mathematics?** This is a description of a process a teacher would use to create an inquiry experience for students. The richness of the student-centered experience in an inquiry classroom is presented through a set of stages with the nuances of the learning process.
- **The Mathematics Rubric**—This rubric is used to analyze student work and thinking based on the NCTM Process Standards.
- **Indicators of Mathematical Thinking**—This supporting document to the rubric was created to help teachers think about developing student mathematical thinking.

CHAPTER 2

- **A Guide to Teaching and Learning Mathematics**—In this chapter, I elaborate on the definition and important components of each of the dimensions of the Mathematical Rubric: problem solving, reasoning and proof, communications, connections, and representations. For each dimension, I provide overall teacher and student goals to guide a reader's understanding and I define several teaching ideas that are essential in instruction. Within the chapter there are also questions, prompts, and suggestions that may be helpful to teachers as they think about, plan, and write lessons and units. It is my hope that this document will be an introductory guide to how to create an inquiry-based mathematics classroom.

CHAPTER 3

• **Examples of Problems, Lessons, and Tasks**—I provide thirty-one model problems, tasks, and lessons to use in the classroom. Many teachers have used these examples successfully. These problems/tasks/lessons are concrete examples of the ideas presented in chapter 2.

CHAPTER 4

• **Guides for Writing Lessons, Units, and Performance Tasks**—I provide a set of guides to help teachers create inquiry lessons, units, and performance tasks. I include sets of questions for teachers to grapple with as they think about engaging students in mathematical ideas and procedures.
• **Big Ideas in Algebra, Geometry, and Probability and Statistics**—Why do we study mathematics? What are the big ideas we want our students to think about? I provide a set of documents to help teachers think about what the big ideas and large questions are within the different branches of mathematics.
• **Questions for Students to Ask Themselves When Solving a Problem**—How do we help students become independent thinkers and doers of mathematics? This guide for students was written to help them think about different questions that will move them to enter into problems with greater ease and be willing to try different approaches to solving problems. My hope is that eventually students will begin to ask themselves these types of questions as they engage in solving problems and learning mathematics.
• **Protocols to Look at Student- and Teacher-Created Work**—I provide a set of protocols that a team of math teachers can use to look at both teacher-created work and student work as a means of informing teaching and learning.
• **Teacher and Student Evaluation Continuums**—I provide a set of continuums for teachers to use to assess how they and their students view the teaching and learning going on in their classrooms. It can be used by teachers to reflect on their craft and to set goals for further growth and development.
• **Evaluation of Teaching and Learning Mathematics at Your School**—I provide a tool based on the *Vision of an Inquiry-based Mathematics Classroom* that a math team can use to assess how the teaching and learning of mathematics are being experienced at their school.

HOW TO USE THIS BOOK

I don't want you to get overwhelmed by the book, and hope that you will engage in its many ideas, problems, and tools. Each of the four chapters in this book includes an introduction to help set up and contextualize the content within the chapter. I do recommend that initially you look closely at chapter 1, as it gives a picture of what I believe should go on in a mathematics class-room. Chapters 2 and 3 can be looked at together, as the ideas presented in chapter 2 are then reflected in real lessons, tasks, and problems presented in chapter 3. Chapter 4 offers many tools that you can use at various times in the school year. I do recommend using the evaluation tools early on in the school year as a means of reflection on what is going on in your own class and all the math classes in your school. This process can be repeated both in the middle of the year and the end of the year as a way of assessing your own develop-ment and the development of the mathematics program in your school.

Most importantly, I want you to see the value in this book and make it part of your teaching and learning. I welcome your comments and questions (JKATZ@ISA-ED.ets.org).

Chapter One

An Explanation of an Inquiry Approach to Teaching and Learning Mathematics

What is mathematics? Why do we teach it? These are the two major questions I ask in my work to help strengthen the teaching and learning of mathematics. I believe the documents in this chapter begin to answer those two questions.

A Vision of an Inquiry-Based Mathematics Classroom is a document that tells the story of what mathematics teaching and learning would be like in a successful classroom. It is theoretical but it is about the real thing. I use as my basis for this vision the National Research Council (NRC) Five Strands of Mathematical Proficiency (NRC 2001). The work done by the NRC was the precursor to the Common Core State Standards along with the National Council of Teachers of Mathematics (NCTM) Process Standards (CCSSI 2010). The NRC document talks about what it means for a student to be mathematically proficient and what we need to do to make that happen. It talks about the deep relationship between conceptual understanding and procedural fluency and how learning one without the other limits real mathematical understanding. It honors the idea that the essence of mathematics is problem solving. And perhaps most importantly, it asks us to think about the productive disposition of each student who comes into our classrooms. Our students enter the mathematics classroom with many years of experiences that affect how they view mathematics. This document will help you to think about how we can begin to help students rethink what is mathematics and how they can feel hopeful and positive about learning this wonderful discipline.

While the *Vision of an Inquiry-Based Mathematics Classroom* describes what is meant by inquiry-based instruction, What Does an Inquiry Process Look Like in Mathematics? gives a detailed description of the inquiry process and helps to illuminate what a student would experience within this type of classroom. The two documents together can support the development of an inquiry-based mathematics program in a school.

A Vision of an Inquiry-Based Mathematics Classroom is about development of deep content knowledge, while the Mathematics Rubric seeks to bridge from the vision to the classroom by focusing on the development of mathematical thinking.

How do we help students develop their ability to think with freedom and flexibility? At the core of developing our students' mathematical thinking are the questions: How do we help students think strategically and with precision? How do we help students reason and defend their ideas? And how do we help students communicate their ideas? This is the essence of the rubric, which I hope will become central to the everyday instruction in your mathematics classroom.

Indicators of Teacher Instructional Practices that Elicit Student Mathematical Thinking and *Indicators of Student Demonstration of Mathematical Thinking* are two documents created to help teachers think about what they will do in the classroom to elicit mathematical thinking and to assess the thinking going on in the classroom. These documents are based on both the *Mathematics Rubric* and *A Vision of an Inquiry-Based Mathematics Classroom*. We believe these documents can be of great use to teachers as they plan lessons/units and facilitate the learning of mathematics in their classroom.

A VISION OF AN INQUIRY-BASED MATHEMATICS CLASSROOM

Imagine a classroom, a school, or a school district where all students have access to high-quality, engaging mathematics instruction (NCTM 2000).

Every student should have the opportunity to go to college and students must have the skills and knowledge necessary for success in college. Thus, it's my hope that schools are thoughtful about creating meaningful college-preparatory instructional programs that make it possible for students to choose college and not have that decision affected by unpreparedness. Mathematics is often a stumbling block and a gatekeeper to students' success in high school and in college (Stinson 2004). In mathematics classrooms, we have an opportunity to raise students' achievement in mathematics by providing students learning experiences that help them make sense of mathematics and understand it in deeper ways. In an inquiry-based classroom students can be successful by learning to reason and think mathematically and apply the ideas of mathematics (Boaler 1987).

This document will present a vision for teaching and learning in an inquiry-based mathematics classroom. I begin by defining what a mathematically proficient student looks like and the specific student behaviors that demonstrate this proficiency. I then discuss what instruction looks like and the importance of students' perceptions of mathematics. I conclude by describing the school leadership's role in guiding schools toward acting on their commitment to graduate every student ready for college.

What Does a Mathematical Proficient Student Look Like?

The NRC convened the Mathematics Study Group to inform our understanding of effective mathematics teaching and learning. The group created a comprehensive view of successful mathematics learning or mathematical proficiency as five interwoven and interdependent strands (NRC 2001):

1. **Conceptual understanding** is the comprehension of mathematical concepts, operations, and relations. It is important to understand that students' conceptual understanding is more than memorization of facts and procedures or knowledge of isolated skills. Students with conceptual understanding also "understand why a mathematical idea is important and the kinds of contexts in which it is useful. . . . Because facts and methods are learned with understanding, they are easier to remember and use, and they can be reconstructed when forgotten" (NRC 2001, 118).

2. **Procedural fluency** involves the skill to carry out procedures flexibly, accurately, efficiently, and appropriately. Procedural fluency has often been viewed as a student who is quick with computation with few or no errors. However, procedural fluency means that students understand when to use certain procedures and how to perform them with flexibility and precision (NRC 2001). A flexible student can use a procedure in different types of problems, including traditional and nontraditional problems; a student who can use only the learned procedure for the type of problem shown in the classroom lacks flexibility as a user of mathematics. Procedural fluency and conceptual understanding are often viewed in school mathematics as competing for attention (NRC 2001) rather than mutually reinforcing. The NRC writes, "[Conceptual] understanding makes learning skills easier, less susceptible to common errors and less prone to forgetting. By the same token, a certain level of skill is required to learn many mathematical concepts with understanding, and using procedures can help and strengthen that understanding" (NRC 2001, 122). For example, if a student understands the notion of "equality," that student would be able to navigate different types of equations with greater ease and would be less prone to error. On the other hand, if a student has the skill to look at pattern relationships within arithmetic procedures, that student will have an easier time generalizing an algebraic concept. This can be seen in the development of concepts with variable manipulation.

3. **Strategic competence** is the ability to formulate, represent, and solve mathematical problems and is similar to what is commonly described as problem solving. In this framework, we see that "students with strategic competence could not only come up with several approaches to a non-routine problem . . . but also could choose flexibly among reasoning, guess and check, algebraic, or other methods to suit the demands presented by the problem and the situation in which it was posed" (NRC 2001, 127).

4. **Adaptive reasoning** is the "capacity for logical thought, reflection, explanation, and justification" (NRC 2001, 116). Adaptive reasoning is essential to a student making sense out of mathematics and seeing it as having a logical structure. The term "adaptive" is used because a proficient student in mathematics has the ability to adapt to the different situations presented in mathematics yet be able to see the connections between mathematical skills and ideas. It is "the glue that holds everything together, the lodestar that guides learning. One uses it to navigate through the many facts, procedures, concepts, and solution methods and to see that they all fit together, in some way that they make sense. In mathematics, deductive reasoning is used to settle disputes and disagreements. Answers are right because they follow from some agreed upon assumptions through series of logical steps. Students who disagree about a mathematical answer need not only rely on checking with the teacher, collecting opinions from other classmates, or gathering data from outside the classroom. In principle they need only check that their reasoning is valid" (NRC 2001, 129).

5. **Productive disposition** is the students' self-perception that they are effective learners of mathematics, their belief in and use of mathematics as a worthwhile endeavor.

The first four strands provide a framework to examine what student behaviors would look like in an inquiry-based mathematics classroom. I will return to the fifth strand later in this section. I envision the students in inquiry-based mathematics classrooms developing these four interdependent strands and being able to

- talk deeply about the meaning of mathematical concepts.
- see the connections and interrelationships between mathematical concepts.
- see the relationship between mathematical concepts and procedures.
- speak about what a procedure means and why it makes sense.
- grapple with all types of mathematical problems.
- see multiple strategies to solve all types of problems.
- defend their process and answer with explanation, justification, and proof.

- critique the reasoning of others and refine their own reasoning on others' feedback.
- reflect on their thinking and learning as a means of self-evaluation and growth as a learner.

Given the behaviors and dispositions, students would demonstrate in a mathematics classroom, it is important to examine what instruction looks like to elicit these student outcomes and what is the role of the teacher in an inquiry classroom.

What Does Instruction Look Like?

Learning mathematics should be a *joyful* experience. The lessons need to be engaging and meaningful, challenging yet interesting. Using an inquiry approach, teachers have the opportunity to create curriculum that makes the classroom an exciting place to be.

In inquiry-based instruction, mathematics is viewed as a humanistic discipline where students construct meaning and understanding within a community of learners (Borasi 1992). It is a multifaceted approach to learning. Students are encouraged to wonder about mathematical ideas, raise questions, make observations, gather data, consider possible relationships and patterns within the data, make conjectures, test one's conjectures, and finally generalize a discovery supported by evidence (Borasi 1992; NRC 1996; Suchman 1968; Wells 1999). Generating an idea or concept and arguing for its authenticity is an essential aspect of inquiry and tells a teacher what a student knows about mathematics (Koehler and Grouws 1992; Lampert 1990).

An essential goal for an inquiry-based mathematics classroom is to help students view mathematics as making sense; thus it is important to help students see that mathematics is based on a structure of patterns. These patterns can help students develop an understanding of the historical development of mathematical ideas. For example, students can learn that the development of irrational numbers arose as the Pythagoreans noticed that in working with a pentagram this oddity occurred with numbers that could not be written as a simple fraction. A pattern led to a conjecture, which eventually led to the creation of irrational numbers.

Asking students to think mathematically is essential to the mathematics classroom. In inquiry instruction, students are asked to think when they grapple with open-ended tasks independently or in collaboration with other students. In developing an understanding of concepts, procedures, rules, and formulas, students are often asked to think about patterns, make conjectures and generalizations, and attempt to prove or disprove them. The thinking can be visual, algebraic, or logical. In all cases, students use their reasoning skills to develop understanding.

The difference between thinking in an inquiry classroom and a conventional classroom is illuminated by the students who experienced the two types of instruction. Two eleventh-grade students, one in an inquiry classroom and the other in a teacher-centered classroom, describe the thinking demands in their respective class. In the conventional classroom, a student describes mathematics as "about replicating." One can understand her notion of mathematics not requiring a great deal of thinking. She states:

> I am forced to think [in math] too, but I already know what I am going to get so I don't have to think as much. In English you have to come up with your own ideas. Before, they used to tell you what you have to write your essay on, and now it is just whatever is in your head. It is hard because you don't know what is there . . . but with math you either got to do this or that. (Katz 2009)

Another student who studied in an inquiry classroom compared his thinking in the two types of classrooms. He states:

> The teachers I had before would just teach math and they would help you write out ways instead of trying to take your time to understand it yourself. Usually they want you to do math just to solve problems . . . [and follow] their way of thinking of math. [My inquiry teacher] wants us to find how we think of math and how we know math. . . . We use our own way of thinking and join [my teacher's] ideas with our own perspective. She wants us to expand our ideas and view other perspectives, including mostly ours. (Katz 2009)

In inquiry classrooms the teachers act as facilitators rather than presenters of knowledge. They will use questions to help students think for themselves and develop their own understandings. They will provide problems that help students develop the skills and abilities to engage with mathematics. In classrooms, the teachers give students multiple opportunities to

- tackle open-ended challenging problems and help them develop strategies and various ways of thinking and approaching the problem.
- construct new knowledge through investigations using interesting tasks and activities.
- become pattern hunters and see the importance of patterns as a means of generalizing mathematical ideas.
- share their conjectures, ideas, and solutions.
- argue about mathematics and defend their ideas with evidence and proof.
- ask questions and work to answer them with the teacher acting as the guide for the students.

- think algebraically and geometrically.
- see that mathematics learning takes place inside the classroom and outside in the world.
- see that mathematics learning is a collaborative endeavor.

Beyond skills and abilities, I return to the fifth dimension of mathematical proficiency offered by the NRC's Mathematical Study Group, *productive disposition*, in order to highlight the importance of students' view of mathematics.

How Will Students Come to View Mathematics?

Students' attitudes, beliefs, and perceptions of mathematics vary greatly in mathematics classrooms. This includes students in both inquiry-based and conventional classrooms (Katz 2009). The fifth strand in mathematical proficiency created by the Mathematics Study Group included *productive disposition*. The Mathematics Study Group described this strand as "the tendency to see sense in mathematics, to perceive it as both useful and worthwhile . . . and to see oneself as an effective learner and doer of mathematics" (NRC 2001, 131). Students "must believe that mathematics is understandable, not arbitrary, that with diligent effort it can be learned and used, and they are capable of figuring it out" (NRC 2001, 131). Students' beliefs and perceptions of mathematics will have a powerful impact on their success; thus it is crucial that mathematics teachers give a great amount of thought to who their students are and how they perceive mathematics.

Students' perceptions of mathematics include their perceptions of the discipline and their perceptions of how they are as learners.

A student with a productive disposition would view mathematics as

- making sense and having a coherent structure.
- a means of solving problems.
- an interesting subject worth the time and challenge to wonder about.
- deeply connected through big ideas.
- an interrelationship between concept and procedure.
- meaningful for their lives.

A student with a productive disposition would view himself or herself as

- capable of doing mathematics.
- capable of thinking and reasoning mathematically.
- capable of solving different types of problems and willing to struggle and persevere.

How Can School Leadership Support This Work?

> In a learning organization, leaders are designers, stewards, and teachers. They are responsible for building organizations where people continually expand their capabilities to understand complexity, clarify vision, and improve shared mental models—that is, they are responsible for learning. (Senge 1994, 340)

A commitment to graduating every student ready for college requires strong instructional leadership. Developing a shared expectation for inquiry teaching and learning, a common belief system, and vocabulary that defines what college-ready behavior looks like, as well as the professional development demands suggest multiple entry points to support this vision. School leaders are the guiding light to facilitate the development of a vision for mathematics in their school and an active partner with their teachers in helping this vision come to fruition. They are supporters and critical friends of the mathematics teachers. They help the teachers create a mathematics vision that organically arises from the vision of the school. Most importantly, the school leaders help the teachers make the vision come alive in an everyday way in the mathematics classroom.

It's important to develop a four-year plan for mathematics to ensure that students have the opportunity to experience a rich, demanding, and exciting mathematics education that prepares them well for college. The work begins with the team of mathematics teachers creating a clear, agreed-upon vision for the teaching and learning of mathematics that defines what you are doing and shapes your actions. The vision identifies what the team hopes the school's math program will accomplish and will guide the school in the creation of a four-year plan for the teaching of mathematics. The plan is detailed, concretely showing how the different outcomes are being developed over four years, from grade to grade, and includes individual units, lessons, activities, performance tasks, and projects. Questions that teams of teachers can think about as they develop this plan are provided at the end of chapter 4 in the Guide to Creating a Vision and Four-Year Plan.

Conclusion

The vision of mathematics education in an inquiry-based mathematics classroom resonates with research and mathematical organizations such as the NRC and NCTM. It is aligned with the Common Core State Standards in Mathematics and it is aligned with the thinking demands that students will encounter in college (Conley 2007). Developing such a program presents challenges and opportunities for teachers and administrators. Ultimately this vision is about our belief in our students and our commitment to help prepare them for life beyond high school.

WHAT DOES AN INQUIRY PROCESS
LOOK LIKE IN MATHEMATICS?

The goal for an inquiry approach to teaching and learning in a mathematics classroom is to help students learn about how they can think about mathematics with a sense of freedom, curiosity, and joy. Paul Lockhart (2012, 6) captures the emotion we want our students to have when they sit in our classrooms.

> What makes a mathematician is not technical skill or encyclopedic knowledge, but insatiable curiosity and a desire for simple beauty. Just be yourself and go where you want to go. Instead of being tentative and fearing failure or confusion, try to embrace the awe and mystery of it all and joyfully make a mess. Yes, your ideas won't work. Yes, your intuition will be flawed. Again, welcome to the club. I have a dozen bad ideas a day and so does every mathematician.

A student in an inner-city eleventh-grade mathematics classroom explains the purpose of creating an inquiry classroom.

> [My inquiry teacher] wants us to find how we think of math and how we know math. . . . We use our own way of thinking and join [my teacher's] ideas with our own perspective. (Katz, 2009)

The process below outlines the stages within an inquiry experience. The order of the stages might change based on the problem, task, or investigation, but the engaging of a student's mind with rich mathematics is always at the core of the experience.

1. **"Play" with the problem.** Students need to feel a sense of freedom when given a problem, task, or investigation that they can go in any direction they choose, even if it is flawed. The goal here is for students to situate themselves within the problem in order to come up with their own ideas so that they can share it with their classmates. As teachers we need to help our students experience that flawed paths can be useful in better understanding the mathematics within the problem, task, or investigation. Student understanding of their own misconceptions can be some of the most important moments in their learning of mathematics. Additionally, the purpose of playing with problems on an ongoing basis is to build perseverance and a willingness to take risks.
2. **Make observations.** Observation is an important skill that is often left out of the math classroom. In an inquiry process, it is crucial to present students with information they can use to begin to make observations. The skill of observation is developed over time. Since students have not

been asked to make observations within mathematics, their observations might start out focusing on unimportant information. As teachers we need to support students to develop as mathematical observers. This will only happen if you give them many, many experiences and have discussions about the observations. If it is a bare number problem, it could be sets of examples where students can observe patterns within the results. If it is developing a concept it could be using real-world representations of the concept (e.g., slope). If it is a contextual problem, the observations can arise from either looking at the given data or creating your own data as a way of analyzing the problem.

3. **Look for patterns**. Mathematics students must understand that mathematics is the science of patterns. Teachers must create experiences where students observe these patterns so they can begin to make sense of an underlying structure that is inherent in mathematical concepts and procedures (see examples 18, 19, and 30 in chapter 3). Building on this idea of patterns helps students to see mathematics as a coherent body of knowledge rather than discrete pieces of knowledge.

4. **Formulate questions**. This stage is very important. The questions will come from the wonderings of students based on their observations and pattern findings. When students begin to form questions, their interest has grown and they want to find out answers to their questions. As teachers, we need to show reverence for students' questions and use them to help guide our planning and teaching.

5. **Make conjectures based on pattern observations or investigations arising from student questions**. Conjecturing is a powerful skill to have. It is a natural process that we do all the time in different situations. Conjectures often can be proven to be incorrect, so it is important for students to know that a conjecture is not a fact. A good example is the Game of 27 (see example 7 in chapter 3). When playing the game, participants are constantly making conjectures about the strategy for winning the game, which they often test out and find their conjecture to be flawed. The engagement of the game propels a person to construct a new conjecture.

6. **Test the conjectures**. Testing is useful when you find a counterexample to disprove your conjecture. When it seems that the conjecture is holding up with different tests, it is crucial to know that we still haven't proven it.

7. **Prove if conjecture holds true all the time**. This is where we move to generalization and fact. Proof can take many forms and it is important that as teachers, we become thoughtful about different ways we can think about proof and support students in that process. "The solution to a math problem is not a number, it's an argument, a proof" (Lockhart 2012, 50).

8. **Conclusion.** What new statement can we make? Is there any new idea we now want to investigate?

MATHEMATICS RUBRIC

This rubric was created so that teachers can begin to assess how their students think when asked to engage in a problematic situation. The NCTM Process Standards reflect five dimensions that are central to student thinking. Thus this rubric should be used when you want to learn about your student thinking. To assess the growth in your students' mathematical thinking over the course of the year, it is recommended that for each student you keep a folder where his or her work on different problems is stored and evaluated using the rubric. In conjunction with this, over the year math teachers should meet together to look at individual student's work to develop a nuanced understanding of how the student thinks about different mathematical ideas. When teachers do this the rubric becomes a continuum of growth for each student and a teacher then can create differentiated experiences for his or her students.

The focus of this rubric is not content knowledge although you can learn about the understanding of content when you assess student mathematical thinking.

Mathematics Rubric

	Beginning Stage	Developing Stage	Proficient Stage	Highly Proficient Stage
PROBLEM SOLVING	No strategy is chosen or a strategy is chosen that will not lead to a solution. Little or no evidence of engagement in the task is present.	A strategy is chosen that is flawed and will not lead to a solution. Evidence of drawing on some relevant previous knowledge is present, showing some engagement in the task.	A correct strategy is chosen based on the mathematical situation in the task. Evidence of applying prior knowledge to the problem-solving situation.	An efficient strategy is chosen and the student progresses toward a correct solution. Adjustments in strategy, if necessary, are made along the way and/or alternative strategies are considered. Evidence of analyzing the situation in mathematical terms. Constructs new mathematical knowledge by extending prior knowledge.
REASONING AND PROOF	The reasoning is unclear or nonexistent.	An argument is constructed with some evidence given. The conclusion is unclear based on the evidence.	Construction of an argument that was not fully supported by the evidence given, leading to a conclusion. The reader needs to infer justification from the evidence given.	Construction of an argument based on evidence, leading to a logical conclusion where there is no need for inference by the reader.

COMMUNICATION	Responses are thorough and well constructed in conveying student's reasoning and process. Communication of an approach is organized, coherent, and efficient, supported by mathematical properties. Mathematical language and symbolic notation are used to consolidate mathematical thinking and to communicate ideas. It could be described as elegant.	Responses are clear and sequenced in conveying student's reasoning and process. Communication of an approach is organized, and coherent. Mathematical language is used throughout the solution to share and clarify ideas.	Responses convey some of student's reasoning and process. Communication of an approach is evident, but it lacks organization and/or coherence. Student uses mostly familiar, everyday language in his/her explanation.	Responses are unclear. Little or no communication of ideas is evident.
CONNECTIONS	Student does all of the following: Student observes and explains coherence between mathematical ideas. Student observes and explains a connection between the task and past experience, past problems, or other subjects.	Student does at least one of the following: Student observes and explains a connection between mathematical ideas. Student observes and explains a connection between the task and past experience, past problems, or other subjects.	Student does at least one of the following: Student observes a connection between mathematical ideas. Student observes a connection between the task and past experience, past problems, or other subjects.	No attempt to connect to mathematical ideas or the attempted connection is inappropriate.
REPRESENTATION	Generalized and accurate mathematical representations are constructed to analyze relationships, extend thinking, and/or interpret thought processes.	Appropriate and accurate mathematical representations are constructed to show growth in thought processes.	An appropriate attempt was made to construct mathematical representations to record thought processes.	No attempt was made to construct mathematical representations or an inappropriate representation was constructed.

Indicators of Instructional Practices that Elicit Student Mathematical Thinking

Indicator	Description	Examples
Classroom Discourse	Classroom discourse consists of any of a variety of exchanges in which ideas about mathematics are communicated within a classroom. As an instructional strategy, this may include dialog between teacher and students, dialog among students, presentations, use of images or diagrams, or any of a host of communicative methods to share mathematical ideas.	1. Teacher communicates expectations for students to explain their thinking process(es) and defend them to one another. 2. Teacher takes a neutral stance, encouraging students to discuss and argue about mathematical ideas. 3. Teacher poses a problem to students and leaves students to their own facility and collaboration to find a solution to the problem. 4. Teacher allows for student-driven discourse in groups.
Open-Ended Questions/Problems	Asking open-ended questions is a key strategy teachers use to stimulate mathematical thinking. Open-ended questions can embody the demand for student exploration, sense-making, application of ideas, extension of ideas, construction of new ideas, connecting ideas to procedures, and struggling with the unknown. Teacher provides for multiple entry points that can lead to one solution or multiple solutions.	Teacher poses questions such as: • Can you explain what you are thinking? • How can we use what we know about working with slope to help us understand the patterns of in/out data tables? Teacher presents a problem such as: • The slope of a straight line changes from 2 to 3. How does that affect its data table of (1,4), (2,6), (3,8)?
"How" and "Why" Questions	Asking "how" and "why" questions gives students an opportunity to describe what they did and why they did it. The students have to be able to give reasons for the choices they made. Reasoning through problems and offering evidence in support of ideas are essential components of mathematical thinking. This leads to the development of student metacognition.	Teacher requires students to support their answers with evidence. • How do you know if your answer is correct? Teacher asks students to describe how they reasoned through a task. • What did you do? • Why did you do it?

(continued)

Indicator	Description	Examples
Mathematical Representation	Mathematical representation refers to multiple ways in which mathematical concepts are presented. Because one specific idea can often be presented in many different forms—in number, in algebraic symbols, in language, in diagram—it is important to the development and expression of students' mathematical thinking for them to understand how they can create mathematical representations to express their mathematical ideas.	1. Teacher records multiple student representations and facilitates discussion about the connections among students' representations. • What is the relationship between the multiple ways we can represent functions? 2. Teacher models her own mathematical thinking through the questions he or she asks himself or herself. 3. Teacher encourages the use of visuals and manipulatives so students can think about a problem or concept.
Use of Contextual Problems	A central rationale for teaching mathematical thinking is that it is necessary in the world beyond the classroom. The world beyond the classroom includes real-life situations that present mathematical problems as well as natural occurrences of mathematics in the world.	Marissa went to a party at her friend's house. She promised her strict father that she would get home by 11 p.m. He told her that she would be grounded for a month if she comes home one second past 11. Was she grounded? Here is some information to help you figure this out. • She left the party at 10:00 p.m. • She drove an old Buick that made a lot of noise as she drove it. • She lived 21 miles from where the party was held. • She drove at the same rate the whole way home. • Marissa was 15.5 miles from home after 16 minutes.

Indicators of Student Demonstration of Mathematical Thinking

Indicator	Description	Examples
Reasoning and Evidence	Reasoning is the capacity for logical thought, explanation, and justification. Students reason through problems and offer evidence in support of ideas. An aspect of reasoning is reflection. Students reflect on their own thinking, looking at whether their approach is sensible or if there is a need for self-correction.	Examples of students demonstrating reasoning and evidence-giving behaviors includes explaining their reasoning process, giving numerical, algebraic, or geometric proof, and giving visual evidence of a correct answer. Examples of student reflection behaviors include students justifying a claim, refuting a claim of a classmate, correcting their own claims, and investigating a new claim proposed by a classmate.
Observing, Conjecturing, and Generalizing	Thinking mathematically consists of making observations of available information, making conjectures about possible solutions to problems, and generalizing from a set of particular cases to formulate new concepts/prodedures for future application.	Students observe different patterns within a set of data, look for relationships within the data, and attempt to conjecture a possible general idea. They test their conjecture for its validity and work to prove the conjecture leading to a generalization. See pages 108–109 for questions that could be helpful for students.
Making Connections	New mathematical concepts make sense to students as they are connected to the other ideas students have already learned. Students make connections around big ideas in mathematics and construct new knowledge by making connections to the knowledge they already have.	Students observe and explain coherence between mathematical ideas and between ideas and procedures. Students observe and explain a connection between the task and past experience, past problems, or other subjects. Students use knowledge or other mathematical understandings to develop a new understanding. See pages 108–109 for questions that could be helpful for students.

(continued)

Indicator	Description	Examples
Strategizing	Students with strategic competence not only come up with several approaches to a nonroutine problem . . . but also choose flexibly among guess and check, algebraic approaches, or other methods to suit the demands presented by the problem and the situation in which it was posed.	Students choose a correct and efficient strategy based on the mathematical situation in the task. Students show evidence of applying prior knowledge to the problem-solving situation. Students show flexibility of mind by being able to rethink strategies while solving a problem. See pages 108–109 for questions that could be helpful for students.
Communication	Students organize and consolidate their mathematical thinking through communicating their mathematical thinking coherently and clearly to peers, teachers, and others; analyze and evaluate the mathematical thinking and strategies of others; use the language of mathematics to express mathematical ideas precisely.	Students communicate through verbal/written accounts using familiar, everyday language and formal mathematical language. Students communicate their thinking and reasoning through use of diagrams or mathematical symbols.
Representation	Students create and use representations to organize, record, and communicate mathematical ideas; select, apply, and translate among mathematical representations to solve problems; and use representations to model and interpret physical, social, and mathematical phenomena.	Students represent mathematical concepts and ideas using diagrams, tables, and mathematical symbols. Students are able to translate from one type of representation to another.

Chapter Two

A Guide to Teaching and Learning Mathematics Using the Five Dimensions of the Mathematics Rubric

INTRODUCTION TO THE FIVE DIMENSIONS

In this chapter, you will find a set of documents based on the five dimensions of the mathematics rubric that will give you many ideas and suggestions of how to create an inquiry-based mathematics classroom. Each dimension has been defined and accompanied by recommended instructional goals that are supported by "best practice" teaching ideas. These five dimensions are a means by which students engage in a true mathematical process. Research supports that constant ongoing engagement with these five critical tools of mathematical thinking leads to greater success in student development of mathematical understanding (Senk and Thompson 2003). An in-depth look at this chapter will enrich both your understanding of good instruction and your students' experience in the mathematics classroom.

Dimension 1: Problem Solving

Problem solving is the essence of mathematics (Hersch 1997). In the Common Core Standards of Practice, the first standard states that students should "make sense of problems and persevere in solving them" (2011, 6). This section can help you to make problem solving come alive in your classroom. As you read through Dimension 1, consider the importance of choosing the appropriate task, the value of encouraging multiple approaches, the meaning of process, the use of error as a tool of inquiry, and encouraging students to create their own problems.

Dimension 2: Reasoning and Proof

In Reasoning and Proof, the thinking processes that help students reach valid conclusions is outlined. This includes observation, conjecture, test of conjecture, and proof. Throughout this whole process, students are asked to reason and justify so they can "construct viable arguments and critique the reasoning of others" (CCSSI 2011, 6). Essential to the success of this process are the development of metacognitive skills where students learn to ask themselves questions that will further develop their ability to think mathematically.

Dimension 3: Communication

In Communication, you are encouraged to use oral and written representations in the mathematical classroom. Teachers can use journals, short-answer questioning techniques, or open-ended problems that will enhance the ability of the students to frame their ideas and questions. This can include students defending their thinking and reasoning in longer, essay-type documents and/or orally in front of a panel of questioners.

Dimension 4: Connections

In Connections, you are encouraged to "bring to life" student interaction with mathematics by drawing on their natural curiosity through the big ideas and essential questions in mathematics. Linking broad mathematical ideas with students' own experience and meaningful investigations will enable students to grasp the concepts that foster procedural fluency and ultimately the deep coherent structure within mathematics.

Dimension 5: Representation

In Representation, an important idea is looked at about how students can learn to express themselves through representations and how they move between different representations within problem-solving situations.

DIMENSION I: PROBLEM SOLVING

Defining a Problem

A problem is any situation, task, or question that students find interesting and challenging (Hiebert et al. 1997). Problems can be procedural, conceptual, and/or they may center on a real-world situation. A problem presents a new situation to students where they have to construct new knowledge and/or apply prior knowledge. This differs from an exercise, which asks a student to replicate a procedure he or she was already shown.

Goal(s) of Problem Solving

Teachers:

Since problem solving is the essence of mathematics, teachers should use problems as an entry point to help students learn new ideas, construct new knowledge, and connect concepts with procedures or an application to a learned idea.

Students:

Students are encouraged to learn, construct, connect, and apply knowledge and/or mathematical concepts to solve problematic situations.

Teaching Ideas in Problem Solving

1. Choose the appropriate problem/task.
2a. Use problems that can be solved with multiple strategies.
2b. Select and apply an appropriate strategy to find a solution.
3. Value process in addition to the answer.
4. Answer student questions in ways that foster understanding.
5. Use error as a tool of inquiry.
6. Have students create their own problems based on their experience with solving different problems.

Teaching Idea #1: Choosing the Appropriate Problem/Task

Teaching Idea	Questions/Prompts	Suggestions
Please take some time while preparing your lesson or unit to think about which problems are appropriate. Please think about what makes a problem appropriate. For example: There are entry points for all students.	For Teacher: Think about the following set of questions when choosing problems for students to attempt: What is the important mathematical idea you want your students to think about?	You must engage with and think deeply about the problem you will be giving to the students. This will help you enormously in preparing your lesson. Anticipate where students will struggle, what misconceptions they might bring to the problem, and what questions you would
The problem is mathematically rich: new concepts and/or procedures are embedded within the problem/tasks. For further commentary on what's meant here see Teaching Idea #3 in Connections on page 50. The task is open-ended, meaning that there are multiple ways for a student to solve the problem. The problem asks students to construct new knowledge.	Why do you think it is an important idea? What new understandings do you want your students to leave with after engaging with the problem? Will the chosen problem make that happen? What was your experience when engaging with the task? What different approaches did you notice that one can take to solve the problem? How can that help you in planning the lesson using the problem? Will the chosen problem interest the students? Why?	ask to help them further engage in the task. Anticipate what different approaches students might take in trying to solve the problem. These following tasks support the idea of student construction of new knowledge. *See example 17 on page 73.* *See example 18 on page 74.*

Teaching Idea #2a: Use Problems with Multiple Strategies

Teaching Idea	Questions/Prompts	Suggestions
Most problems can be solved in different ways. If we give students an exercise in which we ask them to replicate a modeled procedure, we will tend to see most students attempt to do the same thing. If we challenge students with a problem proportionate to their knowledge and ask them to think in a new way about a concept or a procedure, we will see different approaches to solving the problem and we will learn a great deal about our students' thinking. As teachers, we need to permit/encourage students to approach problems in ways they choose. If we require a particular approach we are inhibiting student thinking and the construction of new knowledge. An additional result of enforcing one approach is that we limit the flexibility of thought that is inherent to problem solving, and students feel lost if they don't understand that one approach. When students select inefficient ways for solving a problem we need to not rush them out of that. The inefficiency is part of the process and will soon enough present you with an opportunity to help them rethink their strategy. It's the sense of inefficiency that makes an alternative strategy all the more appealing.	For Students: How else can you do this? Did anyone do it differently? What can you learn from the different approach? Why did you solve the problem in the manner you chose? Do you see a connection between the different approaches your classmates have proposed? Did you try an approach that didn't work? Why didn't it work? Did you follow up with trying a new strategy? If you did, what happened? What did you learn from this experience? For Teacher: How can you help students look at the different approaches to see their connections and find the value in each approach?	Anticipate the various strategies students might use to solve a problem or task. Your ability to do it will be greatly enhanced by your own experience with the problem. To produce multiple strategies, teachers are encouraged to let students "play with the problem" in any way they choose. The teacher can then use the different strategies students thought about as a means of getting all students to further develop their strategic competence. *See example 1 on page 61.* *See example 10 on page 65.*

Teaching Idea #2b: Supporting Students in Selecting and Applying an Appropriate Strategy

Teaching Idea	Questions/Prompts	Suggestions
There are a set of powerful strategies that can help students become better problem solvers if they are given multiple experiences using them: a. Simplifying a problem b. Recognizing a pattern c. Working backward d. Creating diagrams, tables, charts to organize data visually and to observe patterns. The examination of problems can lead to students connecting that problem to previous experiences with problems or to other prior knowledge. Encourage students to articulate the connections they make and have them evaluate which of these connections will help solve a particular problem. To support students in selecting and applying appropriate strategies, have students: • Learn to read a problem for understanding. • Connect the problem to other problems they have experienced, strategies they have used in different problems, ideas in math this problem might be asking them to think about, and procedures that might be used to solve the problem.	For Students: What does the problem ask you to find out? What do you already know or can already do? Does this problem remind you of other problems you have seen? What strategies can you use to solve the problem? How can you make it a simpler problem? How can you use what you observed in the simpler problem and transfer that observation to the more complex problem? How can you organize the information in the problem? Can you use a table or diagram to help you solve the problem? What patterns do you see? What do you observe about the patterns? How can you use the patterns to help to solve the problem? Can you make a conjecture? Can you test it for its validity?	Provide students with multiple experiences with various types of problems, which will encourage them to use different types of strategies. Problem solving needs to be embedded in all units. To transition students into a problem-solving culture, you may begin the school year with a problem-solving unit that gives students multiple opportunities to learn and grapple with different strategies. Later units will use problems as an entry point to think about different concepts and procedures. The goal in this work should be to help students become independent problem solvers. So early on we might scaffold the process for students, but over time the scaffolding should disappear and the students should be able to solve the problems as they are. The danger with scaffolding is that it becomes a set of steps to follow and is not encouraging the development of mathematical thinking. Note on the strategy of simplifying a problem: George Polya (1945) stated that the strategy of simplifying a problem can be a strategy used to solve

(continued)

Teaching Idea	Questions/Prompts	Suggestions
• Decide on a strategy. Assess/test their strategy. Reevaluate their strategy if it does not help them answer the question. • Communicate a strategy in various ways including in diagrams, tables, graphs, etc.	(More questions for students to ask themselves while problem solving can be found on pages 108–109.)	any problem. If you know how to solve a simpler problem you can transfer that knowledge to a more complex problem. *See example 12 on page 68.* *See example 26 on page 82.*

Teaching Idea #3: Value Process and Answer

Teaching Idea	Questions/Prompts	Suggestions
While the answer is important, the development of mathematical understanding requires students to think about what they are doing and why they are doing it. If we view mathematics as being just about skills and procedures, then focusing on the answer becomes central. However, if we believe that the essence of mathematics is problem solving, which includes understanding the inherent relationship between concept and procedure, then the process of problem solving and thinking about ideas becomes central to our instruction. The depth of understanding comes from the process and not the answer. For students to develop deep understanding, we need to honor the process that students are engaged in within their minds. As teachers, we need to be patient and give students time in their development as mathematical thinkers. How and when should we enter into a students' thinking? When do we leave them alone and when do we become part of their thinking process?	For Students: What are you doing? Why are you doing it? Why did you do it? Why does this approach make sense to you? Is there another approach you could have tried? How are the different approaches related to each other?	Here is a set of questions for teachers to think about as they support student development of mathematical thinking. What are the right question(s) to ask that will help my students deepen their thinking about the process without telling them what to do? Have I thought deeply enough about the problem, concepts, and/or procedures I want my students to engage in? Have I thought sufficiently about the task so that I am prepared with different questions to help students enter into the process? What can I learn as a teacher from the different processes students use? What do students learn as they look at their own process? How can I use the different processes to help students think about mathematics with greater conceptual understanding and procedural flexibility? *See example 2 on page 62.* *See example 3 on page 62.*

Teaching Idea #4: Answer Student Questions to Foster Understanding

Teaching Idea	Questions/Prompts	Suggestions
If we respond to student questions with probing questions that help students reason about the problem and grasp the concepts or ideas in the problem, then we are fostering understanding and honoring process. If a student asks a question and we give the answer or show the student what to do, are we fostering understanding or are we reinforcing some procedure, formula, or rule that the student doesn't understand? How do we ensure that what we say to students will push them to think more deeply? As teachers, we might think that we need to relieve the students from their frustration and thus tell them what to do. But when that happens, student thinking often comes to a halt and the students just write the answer down on their paper. Might it be more useful to answer students' questions with questions that guide them and enhance their thinking and understanding?	For Students: What is the problem about? What are you trying to find out? Does this problem remind you of any problem we have done before? How can that help you? Can you simplify the problem? How? Can a diagram help you understand the problem? Can you create a table to help organize the information and use it to look for patterns? Can you make any conjectures? What are they? Are they valid? How can you find out? Can you make any conclusions? How do you know if your conclusion is correct?	Allow students to grapple with problems. Dealing with frustration is part of the process of becoming a good problem solver. How do you encourage students when they are struggling with a problem without showing them what to do? Good questioning of students comes from listening closely to our students' questions and formulating a question or set of questions that will help students engage more deeply in the problem. *See example 4 on page 63.*

34

Teaching Idea #5: Using Error as a Tool of Inquiry

Teaching Idea	Questions/Prompts	Suggestions
Errors provide a great opportunity to discuss and develop conceptual and procedural understanding. Through an inquiry process, student misconceptions can be observed and discussed in terms of procedural development and conceptual understanding.	For Students: Does anyone disagree/agree with the process and solution? Why do you disagree/agree? How might you have done it differently?	Let students wonder about their work; do not rush to correct mistakes. Self-correction is more valuable than teacher correction. When you question students, the purpose should be to have students reflect on their process and thinking.
In the problem below, students are asked to consider a common error in solving equations. Through this task, students can deepen their understanding of "equality," the meaning of zero, and the multiple ways one can solve an equation.	Why did you do that? Does your strategy/solution make sense? Why? Can you show/prove that the solution is correct or incorrect?	*See example 5 on page 63.*

Example Problem

John solved the equation in this way:

$$3x = 5x - 4$$
$$-3x \quad -3x$$
$$\overline{\quad 2x = -4}$$
$$x = -2$$

Do you agree or disagree with John's method/solution? Why or why not?

Teaching Idea #6: Students Create Their Own Problems

Teaching Idea	Questions/Prompts	Suggestions
When students engage in the process of creating their own problems and show ways to solve those problems, they develop a higher level of mathematical understanding.

For example, when studying inequalities, students can see when shown real examples that inequalities are part of their everyday life. So, if we asked students to express mathematically, "You have to be at least 5 feet tall to go on the ride at Great Adventures," they see the inherent connection between the world they know and a mathematical idea.

Then we go a step further and have the students create their own mathematical situation or problem based on their known world. | For the Teacher:

Why do you want students to create their own problems?

What do you hope they/you learn from this experience?

How will you support student success in this task? What questions will you ask them to support their conceptual and procedural understanding so they can be successful in creating the problem? | Be clear about the goal of the activity. If we are looking for understanding, we need to be exact about what that understanding is. Then we can make the assignment clearer to students.

This task may require one-on-one work with students to probe their conceptual and procedural understanding and prod them to go deeper.

When looking at student-created problems, think about what understandings the student had in order to create the problem. (Look for levels of sophistication; ideas, concepts, and procedures embedded in problems.)

See example 6 on page 64.
See example 14 on page 71. |

DIMENSION II: REASONING AND PROOF

Defining Reasoning

Reasoning is used to reach a conclusion.

Reasoning encompasses the tools, skills, and ideas associated with each of the other dimensions of the mathematics rubric.

Defining Proof

Proof is the cogency of evidence that compels the acceptance or establishes the validity of a fact, statement, truth, or conclusion.

Goals of Reasoning and Proof

Teachers:

Providing mathematical explanations and justifications should be a consistent part of a student's experience in the classroom. Thus, teachers must build these opportunities into their daily lessons.

With daily demands to explain and justify, teachers should help build students' capacity to approach new, unfamiliar problems. This is the essence of mathematical thinking.

It is essential that teachers create opportunities for students to engage in inductive as well as deductive reasoning.

Mathematics, as taught traditionally, has students develop deductive reasoning mainly by using two-column proofs in geometry. However, to develop as mathematical thinkers, it is important that students become inductive thinkers.

Students:

Students should acquire and demonstrate competent and proficient mathematical reasoning skills and abilities.

Students should provide evidence for all mathematical conclusions and justify any mathematical reasoning.

Teaching Ideas in Reasoning and Proof

1. Conjecturing
2. Encouraging the use of evidence and proof in daily problem solving
3. Developing students' metacognition.

Teaching Idea #1: Conjecturing

Teaching Idea	Questions/Prompts	Suggestions
Conjecturing and making judgments are part of everyday life. For example, as a teacher, have you ever conjectured about a student's behavior based on immediate observations? Sometimes our conjectures are validated over time and sometimes our conjectures are proven wrong. Students do the same thing. In mathematics we want to see how we can use the skill of conjecturing to promote student engagement and reasoning through exploration of concepts and procedures and engagement in problematic situations. A useful sequence to support students development of their reasoning skills is: • Observe • Look for patterns • Make conjectures • Test the conjectures This process of reasoning aligns with the work of mathematicians who have spent hours looking to prove conjectures.	For Students: What did you observe or notice? Describe any patterns you see. Use your observed patterns to make a conjecture. What is your reason for making that conjecture? Can you test your conjecture to see if it is valid? Can you prove if it is always true? What conclusions can you make based on the proven conjecture? Can you make a prediction based on the proof?	Observing, finding patterns, and conjecturing are all part of the inquiry process. Students need multiple experiences with this process. They need to be left alone or with a partner to grapple with the observed data so they can begin to make conjectures that will eventually lead to new discoveries and construction of new knowledge. *See example 7 on page 64.* *See example 8 on page 65.* *See example 15 on page 71.* *See example 18 on page 74.*

38

Teaching Idea #2: Evidence and Proof

Teaching Idea	Questions/Prompts	Suggestions
We encourage the use of evidence and proof in daily lessons, as it is crucial for the development of mathematical thinking. Providing proof and justifications are an everyday part of the mathematics classroom through answering basic questions about how a problem can be approached and why a solution works (or not). Offering these kinds of evidence makes the process of reasoning apparent to students and teachers. Effective proofs and justifications for conjecture/answer should include: 1. Clear articulation/demonstration of patterns. 2. Clear description of reasoning. 3. Clear examples, possibly addressing counter-examples. 4. Work or explanation showing that students are building off already-known mathematical principles and other knowledge. 5. Generalizations and applications to other cases. 6. Multiple solutions to a problem.	All student explanations should answer these three questions: What did you do? Why did you do it? Can you justify it? Does your solution make sense? Why or why not? Other questions to ask students when discussing their problem solving approach: Why did you choose this strategy? Is there another strategy that could have been used? Can you explain it? Do you see a connection between the different strategies? How do you know your answer is correct? What questions would you ask someone who is struggling with the problem?	In an inquiry mathematics classroom justification with evidence is part of students' daily experiences. They expect the teacher to ask questions like, "Why?" or "How do you know you are correct?" You are encouraged to work toward making this part of your classroom culture. In helping students develop an understanding of the inquiry process, you need to give students multiple experiences where they go from identifying a pattern to making conjectures to generalizing an idea or solution. For students to show why their solution or generalization makes sense, they need to use informal and formal proofs. How can you use informal and formal proof in your classroom teaching? *See example 9 on page 65.* *See example 11 on page 67.* *See example 31 on page 88.*

Teaching Idea #3: Metacognition

Teaching Idea	Questions/Prompts	Suggestions
Metacognition is at the heart of mathematical thinking. Metacognition is the ability to reflect on your own thinking. A metacognitive student is able to ask himself/herself probing questions while working on mathematical problems or tasks. These questions could include: • Am I on the right track? • Does my thinking make sense? • Where am I going? • Should I try another strategy. • Is this question connected to another question I've seen before? A continued posing of questions to oneself builds the capacity for metacognition.	Additional questions students might ask themselves: What would be a reasonable solution to this problem? Why? Where am I going with this problem? Does my strategy make sense? Should I change my approach or strategy? What can I do differently?	Encourage students to be aware of their own thinking. When they are confused, have them write down when they are confused, questions they might have, and how and why they feel a strategy works. To support student metacognition, it is important for teachers to model their own metacognitive process by showing students what questions they might ask themselves. Hitting a block in reasoning is a "teachable moment." Students can access multiple sources to get over the block—other students, the teacher, texts, etc. The key is developing students' independent ability to recognize their blocks and how to address them. *See example 10 on page 65.* *See example 12 on page 68.*

DIMENSION III: COMMUNICATION

Defining Mathematical Communication

Communicating mathematically means expressing the results of mathematical thinking orally, in writing, or with symbolic representations in a clear, convincing, and precise manner.

Through communication, both written and oral, students will strengthen the capacity to reflect, which supports mathematical understanding (Hiebert et al. 1997).

Goals of Mathematical Communication

Teachers:

Teachers will give students multiple opportunities to demonstrate and communicate their mathematical understandings and misunderstandings.

Teachers will use student communication to inform instruction.

Students:

It is essential that students learn to clearly discuss mathematical ideas and processes, and clarify their understanding for themselves and for others through written and oral forms of communication.

Teaching Ideas in Communication

Writing in mathematics gives students the opportunity to reflect on mathematical concepts and clarify their ideas. Three ways to incorporate mathematical communication are:

1. Use of journals
2. Mathematical research and writing within problems and projects
3. Oral communication.

Teaching Idea #1: Use of Journals

Teaching Idea	Questions/Prompts	Suggestions
Use journals to solidify and synthesize student learning; reflect on learnings or ideas; and segue or connect previous knowledge to new knowledge and strategies. Journals can be used at the beginning of a lesson, throughout the lesson to reflect on mathematical ideas or problems, or at the end of the lesson. With journal prompts, students can slowly be guided to learn to justify their ideas, proofs, reasoning, and solutions. Journals may also be used to help students develop multiple perspectives or strategies. Journals may be used to initiate a personal dialogue between teacher and student and provide effective means of formatively assessing understanding.	Possible Prompts for Journal Writing: Explain the (math concept) that was learned yesterday. Where else have we seen this idea or concept before? How is it similar to what I am doing now? What are your lingering questions about this concept? How else might you solve this problem? Describe all the strategies I have used so far to solve the problem. How are these strategies different from one another? How are they similar? Which strategy works best? Why?	Its important that teachers take time to respond to students' journal responses. If there are no responses to journals, journals lose their impact as a tool for mathematical communication. Sticky notes in their journals can be a good way to interact with students in their journals without interfering with their writing space. Additionally, honor their intellectual efforts and pose other questions for them to consider. Journals can be a place for students to reflect on their learning of mathematics. The hope is that the journal will become a place where students automatically go to write when they are confused and when they have made a connection between a mathematical concept and something in another class or something in the real world.
Writing, in any classroom, takes time to develop and especially in mathematics where students may not be accustomed to formulating and expressing their thinking. Think about what you want your students writing to be like in your classroom at the end of the year and what growth toward that would look like. How could	Will this strategy always work? How do I know? Explain how and why this solution works. What questions arise for me? What confused me?	It's best to plan out the journal questions in advance. Doing so will give you time to ensure the wording is the way you want it and that the question addresses what you want. You may find it helpful to keep track of the questions you create and write a small general summary of the types of responses you got from

42

(continued)

Teaching Idea	Questions/Prompts	Suggestions
using the Connections, Representations, and Reasoning and Proof aspects of the rubric help inform how you think about this? How will you communicate the growth you want to see in your students?		your students. Over time this practice could help you begin to craft better questions.

Teaching Idea #2: Mathematical Research and Writing within Problems and Projects

Teaching Idea	Questions/Prompts	Suggestions
A writing portion should be added within a project or open-ended problems so students can: • Explain their thinking process. • Fully describe their problem-solving process. • Explain their solution and why it works. Projects may include research where a student must probe deeper into a mathematical idea or prove a mathematical idea.	Some suggestions for students writing within projects Describe the problem to be solved. Provide an explanation of how you will approach the problem. Why did you choose this approach? Provide a thorough explanation of how you arrived at a solution. Describe your problem-solving process. • Where did you begin? • What was your thinking process? • What helped you come to a solution? • What obstacles did you come across? • How did you change your strategy? • Where did you get confused? • How did you resolve any confusion or obstacle? • What helped you come to a solution? Explain your solution and why it works. Clearly label your diagrams, graphs, or other visual representations. Clearly define any variables.	Definitions are used a great deal in mathematics classrooms as part of writing and communication. Often they cause problems when the ideas in the definition are not understood. *See example 16 on page 71.* It is recommended that mathematical vocabulary be developed within context. Definitions given to students prior to learning about and exploring a topic or concept may have little meaning to students even after a lesson has been taught (Borasi 1992). *See example 13 on page 68.* *See example 14 on page 71.*

44

(continued)

Teaching Idea	Questions/Prompts	Suggestions
	If an equation was derived, give a detailed account of the derivation.	
	Use appropriate and accurate mathematical vocabulary.	
	Check for spelling, grammar, punctuation, and mathematical mistakes.	

Teaching Idea #3: Oral Communication

Teaching Idea	Questions/Prompts	Suggestions
Communicating orally allows students to clearly exhibit their knowledge of a topic. It also helps to deepen student understanding of the concepts and procedures learned. Teachers should allow students opportunities to engage in mathematical talk around problem solving in small groups, pairs, or within whole-class discussion. This is an opportunity for students to learn to critique the reasoning of others (CCSSI 2011). As the lead facilitator in the classroom, the teacher needs to listen closely to the words of students and that should inform the direction of the lesson and/or discussion.	For students giving a presentation of a solved problem: What is the problem asking? What strategy did you employ? Why? How do you know your solution is correct? What would you do if ___ was changed to ___? (use of supposition) What questions might you ask a classmate who is struggling with the problem? For the Teacher: How are you going to help your students grow as presenters? What considerations should the students be making as they think about their presentation? Students and adults alike, when they use technology in presentations, use the technology as the presentation rather than an aid to the presentation. What should students take into consideration when thinking about the usage of technology in their presentations?	All the ideas discussed in every section need to include communication, where students share their thinking and understanding. There are many ways to encourage discourse and communication in the mathematics classroom. Some of them might be: • Socratic Seminars • Cooperative groups and pairs through inquiry investigations • Student teaching of lesson • Informal class presentation • Student defense in front of panel of adults and students When using one of these events, give thought to your purpose and desired outcomes. Listen closely to your students' comments to inform the direction of the activity. Here are some questions to think about: What outcomes would you like your students to achieve? Will the task lead to those outcomes? Why? If using groups, what would be the appropriate number of students for the task? How do you ensure that all members of the group are engaged?

46

(continued)

Teaching Idea	Questions/Prompts	Suggestions
		Should the groups be heterogeneous or homogeneous? Base this on the task and desired outcomes.
		Are you giving students multiple experiences to talk about their thinking in front of the whole class?
		Are you expecting students to ask questions and critique the reasoning of their classmates?
		How will that be built into the classroom culture?

DIMENSION IV: CONNECTIONS

Defining Mathematical Connections

Mathematics connections involve seeing mathematics as a coherent body of knowledge in which ideas and concepts are bound together through big ideas and a common structure.

A mathematical connection is also seeing the relationship between mathematics and the world one lives in and between mathematics and oneself.

Goals of Mathematical Connections

Teachers:

Since making connections, in whatever form they may take, is crucial for developing mathematical understanding, it is imperative that teachers create numerous opportunities for students to view and experience the connectedness of mathematics through engaging problems, historical anecdotes, and meaningful investigations. Thus, teachers should create mathematics units around big ideas and essential questions.

Students:

Students will see and understand how mathematical concepts are linked and build on one another. Students will also see the interrelationship between concepts and procedures with an understanding of how procedural fluency arises from conceptual understanding. This will help students see that concepts and procedures of mathematics fit together to produce a coherent whole. Thus it is a discipline that makes sense.

Students will see the meaning of mathematics in the world by engaging in interesting contextual problems.

Students will begin to wonder, appreciate, and marvel at the connectedness of mathematics and begin to see it as a creative discipline.

Teaching Ideas in Connections

1. Common structures (e.g., patterns) bind together the multiple ideas of mathematics.
2. The history of mathematics helps students make sense of and appreciate mathematics.
3. Contextual problems are meaningful to students.

Teaching Idea #1: Common Structures (patterns) that Bind Together the Multiple Ideas of Mathematics

Teaching Idea	Questions/Prompts	Suggestions
Common structures such as patterns, problematic situations, and proof are present in all disciplines of mathematics. Big ideas such as the concrete and the abstract in algebra and spatial relationships in geometry unite individual disciplines. Many mathematics students think that mathematics doesn't make sense; it is a confusing bunch of rules, formulas, and procedures. Students often view mathematics as discrete pieces of knowledge disconnected from each other. There is no sense of a common binding structure that ties all these ideas of mathematics together. Meanwhile, mathematicians have described mathematics as "the science of patterns." Patterns are one of those binding structures that help connect the seemingly unrelated ideas in mathematics. Students need to see how mathematical procedures arise out of conceptual understanding. This will help students think about procedures with greater flexibility and less as a set of rules to memorize. Pattern recognition is essential for this process.	For Teachers: Do I think helping students make connections matters? Why? If the answer is yes, how can I help make that an everyday experience? How can I help my students make sense of mathematics? How can I use pattern hunting as an entry point to understanding a new rule, procedure, or formula? Can I create an interesting task to facilitate the making of connections?	Students must have multiple experiences where they look at patterns as a means of making sense of rules, formulas, definitions, and procedures. An essential component when studying functions is the idea that tables of values, graphs, and equations are mathematically identical. We must help students make that deep connection between those three representations. A big idea in mathematics is the notion of ratio. When students have a deep understanding of ratio as inherent to concepts such as slope, trigonometric ratios, pi, and the probability of an event, the students will be able to think about these concepts with greater understanding. When writing a unit, teachers need to ask themselves, "What is the mathematical story I want my students to think about that will help them to focus on the big ideas?" *See example 1 on page 61.* *See example 15 on page 71.* *See example 16 on page 71.* *See example 18 on page 74.* *See example 29 on page 85.*

Teaching Idea #2: The History of Mathematics Helps Students Make Sense of and Appreciate Mathematics

Teaching Idea	Questions/Prompts	Suggestions
All knowledge is evolving and we want students to see that this is true about mathematics itself and about themselves as learners. Using the history of mathematics in the classroom can help students to develop a new understanding of mathematics. Students rarely have a notion that the ideas they are learning have a history; students often think that mathematical ideas just fell from the sky. When we help students see that mathematical ideas and procedures were developed at different points in history because a need arose for these ideas, then mathematics takes on new meaning. For example, a French gambler asked a question to the mathematician, Blaise Pascal, about winning and losing. This led to a famous correspondence Pascal had with the great mathematician Pierre de Fermat that led to the development of probability theory. By helping students understand some of that history, they will see that mathematical ideas, like all ideas, develop over time.	For teachers to think about and research: How did numbers come to be? What made for the development of the zero? How did the development of man's mind lead to the development of the Hindu-Arabic number system? How can I use the story of pi to fascinate students about this amazing number? Why do mathematicians define mathematics as the science of patterns? How do we see that idea in the history of mathematics? How do we see that idea in what we are learning in our classroom?	Look at the history of numbers including Egyptian, Babylonian, Chinese, and Mayan number systems in comparison to the Hindu-Arabic number systems. It would be an opportunity for students to appreciate the power of the number system we use today. We encourage you to read about the history of mathematics. There are wonderful stories you can share with your students that can add to their appreciation of mathematics. *See example 17 on page 73.*

50

Teaching Idea #3: Contextual Problems are Meaningful to Students

Teaching Idea	Questions/Prompts	Suggestions
We are often told that we have to make mathematics relevant to our students' lives. Yet, what does that really mean? We can find in many textbooks "real-world" problems that have no meaning for students and are not "real" to them. What matters most is that we create tasks that are contextually interesting or mathematically interesting for students even if they are not part of students' everyday experiences (Nicol and Crespo 2005). In chapter 3 we have chosen problems that students will feel are relevant to their lives. But we have also chosen problems that students have found interesting and engaging even if they are not seemingly relevant to them.	For Teachers: The task or activity you choose can be purely mathematical (*example 15 on page 71*) or have some context to it (*example 1 on page 61*). The questions below should be considered for both types. Will the task/activity be interesting to my students? Why? What makes the task/activity mathematically meaningful for the students to experience? What do you want to learn about your students' mathematical thinking from this task/activity? What background knowledge will my students need in order to focus on the task or activity? Does the task have multiple entry points?	Students love to play games. There are many games that will engage students to develop concepts in math. We include some of these games in this book. Mathematics is a creative experience. The creation can take place every day when students construct a new idea or procedure, find an interesting path to solving a problem, or create a physical model to represent a real-world structure. Students love to create. Some of these can take the form of projects. There are many opportunities in mathematics for students to apply mathematical ideas through these projects. See *example 7 on page 64*. See *example 22 on page 77*. See *example 27 on page 84*. See *example 28 on page 84*.

DIMENSION V: REPRESENTATION

Defining Mathematical Representation

Mathematical representation is any of the myriad ways mathematical ideas may be expressed in writing, orally, or visually (e.g., pictures, graphs, charts, tables, diagrams, symbols, mathematical expressions and statements, etc.)

Goals of Mathematical Representation

Teachers:
  Teachers will help students bridge the concrete and the abstract through the development of multiple representations.
  Teacher will help students understand that algebra is "generalized arithmetic"; thus they can use arithmetic to develop algebraic understanding.
  Teachers will help students learn to analyze different representations of the same situation and see how they are the same (e.g., word, table, graph, and equation).
  Teachers will help students develop the flexibility to use different representations to solve problems.

Students:
  Students will be able to talk about why algebra is "generalized arithmetic" and how to use arithmetic to develop algebraic concepts and procedures.
  Students will be able to use a variety of representations to model, interpret, and extend understanding of mathematical ideas and real-world situations.

Teaching Ideas in Representations

1. Learning to Abstract
   a. Moving from arithmetic to algebra
   b. Using concrete structures or examples of concrete structures to have students examine mathematical ideas
2. Making sense of confusion to solve problems
3. Using mathematical representations to interpret, explain, and justify
4. Mathematical Modeling
   a. Modeling mathematical ideas and real-world situations
   b. Projects of the world that use rich mathematics

52

Teaching Idea #1a: Moving from Arithmetic to Algebra

Teaching Idea	Questions/Prompts	Suggestions
Algebra has been defined as "generalized arithmetic." It is essential for teachers to help students use what they know within arithmetic to begin to generalize mathematical ideas. Teachers can use many examples of specific cases then have students see that through algebra we can create one general case that stands for all cases. The variable becomes the tool we use to create these generalizations. Thus we are helping students move from arithmetic to algebra. Pattern recognition is essential if students are to make connections between the concrete and the abstract or the specific cases and the general case. It is the patterns students understand that will help them to make algebraic generalizations. We see an example of using arithmetic to develop algebraic thinking with the *Cows and Chickens* problem below. See how we can use guess and check, a wonderful strategy using arithmetic understanding to lead to an algebraic approach to problem solving.	For Students: • Look at the arithmetic examples given to you. Describe what you notice. • What patterns do you see? • Can you take the specific examples and write one sentence that describes all the examples? • Can you write an algebraic expression that can describe all the specific examples?	Use as one of your year-long essential questions: "How is algebra generalized arithmetic?" In developing conceptual understanding and procedural fluency, it is of great importance that you help students develop both the concept and the procedure from the patterns of arithmetic. See example 18 on page 74 to learn how conceptual procedural understanding can be developed from arithmetic patterns. *See example 19 on page 75.* *See example 30 on page 86.*

Teaching Idea	Questions/Prompts	Suggestions
While it is recommended you start with a simpler problem to develop this algebraic approach from an arithmetic approach this problem was chosen because of its richness and clarity of connections between arithmetic thinking and algebraic thinking.		

Example Problem: Cows and Chicks

Farmer Jose has a farm in upstate New York with cows and chickens. Jose is forgetful. His worker, who likes to count odd things, told him that he has a total of 50 cows and chickens that combined have a total of 124 legs. But neither of them were sure how many were chickens and how many were cows. Your task is to find this out for them.

Teacher: Let students play with this any way they want. If they are struggling, recommend to them that they organize this into a table with headings "# of Cows," "# of Chickens," and "Total # of Legs." They can use intelligent guess and check.

# Cows	# Chickens
20	30
10	40
12	38

Question for the teacher: How can we use this to develop an algebraic approach?

Questions for students: If you chose 20 cows, how did you find out the number of chickens? If you chose 10 cows, how did you . . . ? If you chose "x" cows, how would you represent the number of chickens? (x and 50-x).

# Cows	# Chickens	Total # Legs
20	30	140
10	40	120
12	38	124

Question for teacher to ask: How did you get the total number of legs?

You want students to talk about multiplying the number of cows by 4 and the chickens by 2.

So the equation could become $4x + 2(50 - x) = 124$.

54

Teaching Idea #1b: Using Examples of Physical Structures

Teaching Idea	Questions/Prompts	Suggestions
It is recommended that teachers use physical examples to help students connect the abstract to the concrete. Many students find it difficult to think abstractly. One way to help students enter into that world is by using concrete examples from the world to talk about the abstract idea. You might look at the idea of steepness in terms of mountain and steps to help students move toward the idea of slope. Which mountain or steps would be harder or easier to climb? How can you translate that idea to lines on a coordinate plane?	For the Teacher: How is the topic I am teaching connected to the real world? What mathematical ideas do I see reflected in the world around me? How can I use the concreteness of physical structures to help students understand abstract ideas? Can a graphical representation help me to solve the problem?	Begin the study of a particular unit by showing pictures of the phenomena being studied (e.g., arches, bridges, trajectory of a ball for quadratic functions, speed limit signs for inequalities, steps and ramps for slope). You can use those photographs to begin to develop the mathematical concept. *See example 10 on page 65.* *See example 20 on page 75.* *See example 21 on page 76.*

Teaching Idea #2: Making Sense of Confusion to Solve Problems

Teaching Idea	Questions/Prompts	Suggestions
Students often encounter problems when they don't understand what they are being asked to find out. We need to help them find ways to lessen the confusion and begin to make sense of the problematic situation. It is important that students experience problems that use different strategies and can be represented in different ways. They could include: • Drawing a diagram. • Organize the information in a table. • Simplify the problem. • Look for patterns. • Work backward. • Use an algebraic approach.	For Students: Can I draw a picture to help me better understand the problem? Can I create a table to help me organize the information? Can I simplify the problem using small numbers to help me understand the problem? Can I look for a pattern to help me make sense of the problem? Can I solve this problem using an algebraic approach?	To become better problem solvers, students need to have many experiences with different types of problems. Students need to experience different strategies that use different types of representations where over time they become part of students' repertoire of ways to solve a problem. Teachers need to model the questions they ask themselves when solving a problem. A goal is to help students learn to ask themselves those questions. *See example 26 on page 82.*

Teaching Idea #3: Interpreting and Explaining

Teaching Idea	Questions/Prompts	Suggestions
It is important that students have the chance to represent ideas, thinking, and solutions in multiple ways. They can use graphs, tables, mathematical statements, pictures, symbols, animation, skits, poems, prose, and diagrams (i.e., Venn Diagrams). You can learn about your students' understanding of geometric figures by asking them to create a skit (with a partner) whose main characters are two geometric shapes. Each partner takes on one shape and tries to show why his shape is unique. They could act out the skit and other students in the class can try to discover which figures are being described. Students should have the experience of using math representations to teach a concept/idea to each other, teachers, family members, and younger students.	For Students: How can this (solution, situation, etc.) be represented? What would be the best representation? What does this symbol tell us? How else can I represent this idea? Is there a picture that could represent this idea? Where might I see this outside the class? Can I draw an example of this idea? How can I use the table to describe the equation or the graph? Could I write a story that goes along with a given equation? Table? Would it help to create a rap that shows conceptual and procedural understanding of _____?	As much as possible each unit should have a written, oral, and visual component. Cover walls with a variety of student work demonstrating representations. Have lots of models, manipulatives, and materials for students to work with in developing mathematical representations. Use graphical support as a tool for inquiry. Use the graphing calculator, GeoGebra Geometer's Sketchpad, Cad Cam programs for architectural design, and other mathematical software to help students discover and represent properties of geometric figures and other concepts. Plan trips to art museums (for example, to see Islamic art, Frank Lloyd Wright, rooms from other cultures at the Met) to observe and discover mathematical representations in other cultures.

Teaching Idea #4a: Modeling Mathematical Ideas and Real-World Situations

Teaching Idea	Questions/Prompts	Suggestions
"Mathematically proficient students can apply the mathematics they know to solve problems arising in everyday life, society, and the workplace" (CCSSI 2011, 7). One of the great powers of mathematics is that it gives us the chance to model simple and complex mathematical ideas and it gives us the chance to model real-world situations. Modeling gives us the chance to make sense, give new meaning, and make predictions. Frequently we can make different mathematical models for the same situation. When working with functions, the model can take the form of table, graph, or equation.	For Teachers: How can I help my students model a particular mathematical idea or real-world situation? Why is it valuable to model this particular idea or situation? What do I want my students to think about when they model a particular mathematical idea or real-world situation? How do I help my students think about the relationships between different models?	Using real data to help students model real-world situations is valuable and makes your work authentic. *See example 25 on page 82.* Using real-world data also raises many issues, since the data will most often require student understanding of regression. The patterns that are the essence of mathematics can be modeled in different ways. How can I help students model patterns? We can think about modeling the problem: What is the sum of the first 100 odd counting numbers? First *n* counting numbers? Can you create a visual model to describe the pattern? Can you create an algebraic model of the patterns within the Koch snowflake (fractals)? *See example 22 on page 77.* *See example 27 on page 84.* *See example 28 on page 84.* *See example 29 on page 85.*

58

Teaching Idea #4b: Projects of the World that Use Rich Mathematics

Teaching Idea	Questions/Prompts	Suggestions
We use modeling to help students see the connections between the concrete and abstract and as a means to explain the real world Mathematical representations should be used in order to develop a deeper and richer mathematical understanding.	For Teachers: What understandings will students gain through a modeling project? What do you want students to know and think about at the end of this project? How does the project lead to the development by students of mathematical models?	Ensure the projects are mathematically rich and challenging. They should require students to abstract by developing mathematical models. You are encouraged to use real-world data to help students understand how mathematics can explain phenomena in the world. *See example 22 on page 77.* *See example 23 on page 80.* *See example 25 on page 82.*

Chapter Three

Problems, Investigations, Lessons, Projects, *and* Performance Tasks

It is the questions that drive mathematics. Solving problems and making up new ones is the essence of mathematical life.

—Reuben Hersh (1997)

INTRODUCTION

Researchers differentiate between the concept of a problem and an exercise (Hiebert et al. 1997), as do educators. When I say "problem," I am referring to what's frequently called a nonroutine problem, which calls for a student to make new meaning in a situation that has never been experienced before. On the other hand, in an exercise, the student is asked to use the same thinking and apply the same procedures as recently learned. Both problems and exercises can be contextualized (i.e., real world) or decontextualized (i.e., an equation whose solution requires the application of known procedures). As a result of this distinction, what is often referred to as a "set of problems for practice" I would call "exercises."

There is value in using exercises in instruction, but not as a vehicle for developing new understanding. This is why lessons should begin with a problem or some kind of inquiry activity. When exercises are used they need to be judiciously selected to avoid the passive practice that's frequently associated with them. Students need to be supported to consciously connect the exercises to the underlying concept that's being reinforced. Then, practice with exercise will lead to greater flexibility of thought.

There is a nuance to this that is not immediately apparent and is worth highlighting through an example. The solution of an equation, under different situations, could be a problem or an exercise. For example, if a student were presented with a single variable linear equation with variables on both sides, but had only seen and worked with two-step equations with the variable on one side, it would be characterized as a problem. In this case, the student would have to construct a method for solving the equation. On the other hand, if the teacher had already modeled how to solve this type of equation and the student were practicing the procedure, it would be an exercise.

Notes on the Problems

The following set of problems was culled from many different sources including problems; some are famous problems and others were created by me and my math colleagues. These problems are presented as examples that represent different aspects of the Five Dimensions found in chapter 2. At the top of each problem you will observe the cited teaching idea that the problem was intended to exemplify, though in many cases a problem could model other aspects of the dimensions.

These problems are presented in different ways (an activity, a lesson, a project, or a performance assessment) to show the many forms problems can take. Additionally, many of these problems could be used as on-demand problems, where students work independently for a period and the teacher uses the students' work to understand their thinking, while others lend themselves to working in groups.

Steps to Facilitate Student Perseverance

a. Have students try the problem on their own, see how they approach the problem and where they hit roadblocks.
b. Teacher intervention point: *Determine at which points you will intervene to help facilitate discussion and reasoning. Prior to your intervention consider pairing students up to share their strategizing and thinking with one another.*
c. You might need to help students rethink their strategy by helping them to be metacognitive about what they are doing.
d. Have a classroom discussion about the thinking that went on as students attempted to solve the problem.

A Possible Next Step

If there is a problem you can't solve, then there is an easier problem you can solve: find it.

—*George Polya (1945)*

I encourage you to work the problems and reflect on your process as well as the multiple ways your students may approach and attempt to solve them. Doing the problems has been a great help for teachers over the years. By thinking about the benefits of using problems like these and working through them, you come to see that the problem-solving experience is more meaningful than just getting the answer. To this end, I have provided some questions that may help you get the most out of working through these problems.

What did you notice about your thinking and the decisions you made while working through the problem?
What are other ways one might approach the solution of the problem?
What issues will the problem present to students?
What questions might they ask?
How will you respond to those questions?
How else might you support them?

Finally, as you work through these problems, in following Polya's advice, you should think about this most valuable problem-solving strategy of making a similar *simpler problem*. When you simplify a problem, it is easier for students to make sense of the problem. They can then take that understanding and transfer it to the more complex problem. Many problems lend themselves to use of this strategy. In example 12 on page 68, you are asked to work with one thousand lockers. If students simplify this by looking at what happens with one locker and one person, two lockers and two people, and so on, up to ten lockers, the pattern that expresses itself may become apparent, giving the students the opportunity to transfer that understanding to the situation with a thousand lockers.

EXAMPLE 1: USING MULTIPLE STRATEGIES | LOOKING FOR PATTERNS

Cookie Box Dilemma

I visited friends in New York City during the summer. They took me to this HUGE Save-A-Lot store. There was a display of cookie boxes that I could not believe! The display was in a pyramid shape with at least 100 boxes as the base. I had to stand back and wonder how many boxes were in the whole display. I imagine when they started building the display it might have looked like the pictures below.

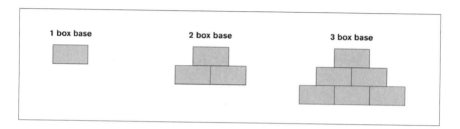

- How many boxes of cookies are in a display with a base of 5 boxes? 10 boxes?
- Can you come up with a rule for finding the number of boxes in a display that has 100 boxes in the base like the display I saw at Save-A-Lot?
- Can you come up with a rule for finding the number of boxes in a display for **any number** of boxes in the base?

EXAMPLE 2: VALUING PROCESS | SHAKIRA'S NUMBER

Shakira is thinking of a number. She said, "When you divide it by 2, 3, 4, 5, or 6, you will have a remainder of 1, but if you divide it by 7 you will have no remainder." What is Shakira's number? Can there be more than one answer? How do you know?

EXAMPLE 3: VALUING PROCESS | CROSSING THE RIVER

There are 8 adults and 2 children who need to cross the river and they only have 1 boat available. The boat can only hold 1 adult or 1 child or 2 children. Everyone in the group is able to row the boat. How many one-way trips will it take for everyone to cross the river?

How many one-way trips will it take for 10 adults and 2 children? 15 adults and 2 children?

Can you design a general rule that would work for any number of adults and 2 children?

EXAMPLE 4: SIMPLIFYING THE PROBLEM | ANSWERING STUDENTS' QUESTIONS TO FOSTER UNDERSTANDING

Checkerboard Problem

Can you find how many squares there are on an 8" by 8" checkerboard?

Can you now find how many rectangles there are on a checkerboard?

EXAMPLE 5: USING ERROR AS A TOOL OF INQUIRY

When Can I Divide?

Tenisha and Jose were given a problem by their teacher. They were asked to simplify a rational expression. In their work, they were left with:

$$\frac{X + 1}{X - 3}$$

Tenisha said, "I think we're finished." Jose said, "No I think we can still simplify." He did the following:

$$\frac{\cancel{x}+1}{\cancel{x}-3} = \frac{1}{-3}$$

Who was correct? Why do you say that?
What happens in this case?

$$\frac{3(x-1)}{4(x-1)}$$

EXAMPLE 6: STUDENTS CREATE THEIR OWN PROBLEMS

Creating a Mathematical Situation: Three Examples

Example #1: Create an equation with the variable on both sides of the equality whose answer is 3. Show that it works.

Example #2: Create a situation using one of the following: at least, at most, minimum, or maximum. Write the situation algebraically, graphically, and in words.

Example #3: Create a real-life situation that is a function. For the situation,

- Define the independent variable and dependent variable.
- Sketch a reasonable graph with explanation.
- Give the approximate domain and range.

EXAMPLE 7: REASONING AND CONJECTURING

The Game of 27

You are going to play a game with the following rules:

- You will be given 27 chips.
- There are exactly 2 players.
- The 2 players will alternate turns.
- At each turn, a player removes 1, 2, 3, or 4 chips from the pile.
- The game ends when all the counters have been removed.

The player who takes the last chip wins the game.

Challenge 1:

Find a strategy that will have you always win the game.
Write down your observations as you play the game.

Challenge 2:

The last person who picks a chip loses the game. Find a strategy that guarantees you always win the game.

EXAMPLE 8: CONJECTURING

The String Problem

Jose and Al are in detention. They are sitting in a rectangular classroom with nothing to do. The classroom floor is 24 square-tiles long and 18 square-tiles wide. Jose says, "If I take a string and stretch it from corner to another corner making a diagonal, how many tiles does the string cover?"

    Note: A string does not cover a tile if it only *touches* the vertex of that tile. (Write down all your ideas, conjectures, and tests of conjectures.)

    Can you generalize for any rectangular room (x tiles long by y tiles wide) whose floor is covered with square tiles?

EXAMPLE 9: CONJECTURING AND PROOF

Congruence and Similarity

We know triangles have 3 sides and 3 angles. What is the least amount of information we need to know to show:

a. That 2 triangles are congruent?
b. That 2 triangles are similar?

What are your conjectures?
How are you going to prove if your conjectures are true?

EXAMPLE 10: METACOGNITION ON MULTIPLE STRATEGIES

The Race

Sitting in his math class, Malik is trying to figure out how he is going to get an A for the year, especially since he has missed handing in so much of the homework. Then, he has a brilliant idea.

    Malik's teacher, Mr. Showoff, is always bragging about what a great runner he was in college and how many trophies he won. So Malik says to his teacher, "I have a cousin who is a pretty good runner. Would you like to race him? He's a little bit younger than you so I bet he would even give you a head start." Malik dares his teacher and says, "If my cousin beats you, you give me an A in math for the year. If you win, I'll make up all my homework and do any extra work that you give me." Malik's teacher thinks for a minute, "After I win, I'll be able to get Malik to catch up on his work." Then he says, "Okay. I'll do it. Who's your cousin?"

Malik: "Usain Bolt."

Teacher: "Usain Bolt! You mean the Jamaican guy who broke world records for the 100 and 200 meter races in the 2008 Olympics?"

Malik: "That's rrriiigghhttt. But you can't back out now."

Teacher: "Okay, I'll do it. But I better get a good head start."

Malik: "Okay. I'll lay out the race for you and I'll make sure you have a good head start."

It is RACE DAY. . . . **When the starting buzzer sounds, Malik's teacher springs from the starting line and tears down the course. Usain takes off some time later.**

NOTE: ALL TIMES ARE GIVEN SINCE THE STARTING BUZZER SOUNDED.

The Teacher:
    15 seconds after the buzzer, the teacher still has 135 meters to go to the finish line.
    32 seconds after he left the starting line, the teacher has only 50 meters more to run.

Usain Bolt (Usain starts running at some point after the teacher starts):
    22 seconds after the buzzer, Usain is 189 meters from the finish line.
    36 seconds after the buzzer, he is 42 meters from the finish line.

BOTH PEOPLE ARE RUNNING AT A CONSTANT SPEED. Your task is to **determine the outcome of the race**. You need to **explain the process that you used** and show all the mathematics.

EXAMPLE 11: EVIDENCE AND PROOF

Whodunit

A person is murdered and the police have put together 22 clues to solve the crime.

Your job as a team is to use the clues to advise the police on following unknown details of the murder.

- Who was the victim?
- Who was the murder? What was his/her job?
- At what time did the murder take place?
- How was the victim killed?
- What was the murder's motive?

Setup

The clues should be a deck of 22 cards all face down. Members of the group should draw one card at a time until all the cards have been given out. Each team member is allowed to share the information on their card(s), but they are not allowed to show other team members their card(s). Groups can be as small as 5, but it is recommended that groups have between 8 and 10 members.

The Clues:

When he was discovered dead, Mr. Johnson had a bullet hole in his calf and a switchblade wound in his back.	Mr. Johnson had been dead for about an hour when his body was found, according to the coroner.
Mr. Johnson's body was found at 1:20 a.m.	Mr. Johnson had wiped out Mr. Blue's business by stealing his customers.
Mr. Blue shot an intruder in his apartment building at midnight.	Mrs. Stevens did not see Mr. Johnson leave through the lobby while she was waiting.
The elevator operator reported to the police that he saw Mr. Johnson at 12:15 a.m.	A switchblade found in the parking garage had been wiped clean of fingerprints.
Bloodstains corresponding to Mr. Johnson's blood type were found in the basement parking area.	Mrs. Stevens had been a good friend of Mr. Johnson and had often visited his apartment.
The bullet taken from Mr. Johnson's calf matched the gun owned by Mr. Blue.	Mrs. Stevens had been waiting in the lobby for her husband to get off work.
Police were unable to locate Mr. Blue after the murder.	Mrs. Stevens's husband had been jealous of the friendship.

Only one bullet had been fired from Mr. Blue's gun.	The elevator operator went off duty at 12:30 a.m.
Mr. Johnson's blood type was found on the carpet outside Mr. Blue's apartment.	Mrs. Stevens's husband did not appear in the lobby at 12.30 a.m., the end of his normal working hours. She had to return home alone and he arrived later.
The elevator operator said that Mr. Johnson did not seem too badly hurt.	Mr. Johnson's body was found in the park.
There were bloodstains in the elevator.	At 12:45 a.m., Mrs. Stevens could not find her husband or the family car in the basement parking lot of the apartment building where he worked.

EXAMPLE 12: METACOGNITION

The Locker Problem

There are 1,000 lockers lined up numbered 1 to 1,000 and there are 1,000 students. The lockers are all closed. The first student, Jasmine, walks by and opens all the lockers. Then the second student, Al, walks by and goes to every second locker starting at #2 and closes it. Then Mary walks by and goes to every third locker starting at #3, closing the opened lockers and opening the closed lockers. The fourth student walks by and goes to every fourth locker starting at #4, closing the opened lockers and opening the closed lockers. This routine goes on until student 1,000, Michael, goes to locker #1,000 and either closes it or opens it. After this is finished, which lockers will be open? Why?

EXAMPLE 13: WRITING IN PROBLEMS

Gaming the Dice

You are going to play a game rolling two dice. You want to keep rolling until you get a sum of 7. You need to record the number of rolls it took to get a sum of 7.

Example:

Dice came up 3 and 2
Dice came up 5 and 4
Dice came up 6 and 2
Dice came up 4 and 3

IT TOOK 4 ROLLS TO GET A SUM OF 7

Before you start the game, predict the average number of rolls it will take to get a sum of 7. Write a sentence explaining your prediction.

_____

_____

You are going to play the game 10 times. Record the number of rolls needed each time to get a sum of 7.

Game #	Number of rolls needed to get a sum of 7
1	
2	
3	
4	
5	
6	
7	
8	
9	
10	

Now find the average number of rolls by adding the number of rolls and dividing by 10.

Did this get close to your prediction? Why do you think this happened?

Now let's see why this happens.

You are going to make a **sample space** showing all the possible outcomes when you roll two 6-sided dice numbered 1 to 6.

I'll get you started and you complete it.

SAMPLE SPACE

1-1	2-1	3-1	4-1	5-1	6-1
1-2					
1-3					
1-4					
1-5					
1-6					

How many possible outcomes are there?

How could you have gotten that answer using the **counting principle? EXPLAIN.**

_____

_____

_____

Now look at your sample space and complete this table.

SUM	# of favorable outcomes	PROBABILITY
1		
2		
3		
4		
5		
6		
7		
8		
9		
10		

Look at your table.
Do you see any patterns? Write down your observations.

Look at the sum of seven on your table. How does the probability compare to what happened when you played the **Game of 7?**

Explain your answer in at least two sentences.

_____

_____

_____

_____

_____

_____

EXAMPLE 14: PROBLEMS ARE MEANINGFUL TO STUDENTS

Does Penelope Crash into Mars?

Penelope is out navigating through space and decides to visit Mars. As she approaches, she changes her mind, decides that she does not wish to visit Mars, and fires her retro-rocket. The spaceship slows down, and if all goes well, stops for an instant then starts pulling away. While the retro-rocket is firing, Penelope's distance, from the surface of Mars is defined by a quadratic function based on the number of minutes since she started firing the rocket. Penelope is tracking her position:

- At 1 min she is 425 kilometers (km) above the surface of Mars
- At 2 mins. she is 356 km above the surface
- At 3 mins. she is 293 km above the surface

Does Penelope crash into Mars? Defend your answer with mathematical evidence including a sketch of Penelope's trajectory.

EXAMPLE 15: PATTERNS AND CONJECTURING

Consecutive Sums Problem

Which counting numbers cannot be written as the sum of two or more consecutive counting numbers?
Can you prove that your findings will always hold?

EXAMPLE 16: STRUCTURES IN MATHEMATICS

Activity to Lead to Definitions of a Relation and a Function
Creating Definition (Algebraic Ideas)

You will be given 10 figures. In your group, classify them in any way you want.

You may put a figure into more than one group. Why did you put them together in these groups?

Chart your findings. Be sure to make clear your explanations as to your groupings.

Each group will present their findings and other groups will ask questions. Through these classifications, can we create a definition for each of the different groups?

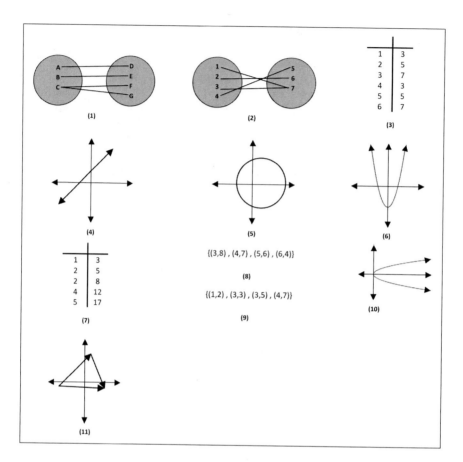

(1)

(2)

1	3
2	5
3	7
4	3
5	5
6	7

(3)

(4)

(5)

(6)

1	3
2	5
2	8
4	12
5	17

(7)

{(3,8) , (4,7) , (5,6) , (6,4)}

(8)

{(1,2) , (3,3) , (3,5) , (4,7)}

(9)

(10)

(11)

EXAMPLE 17: THE HISTORY OF MATHEMATICS

The Pythagorean Triplets

The Pythagorean Theorem has had a wonderful history. The Babylonians and Egyptians clearly showed some understanding of this idea but the credit is given to the great Greek philosopher Pythagoras and his followers who were called Pythagoreans.

The Pythagoreans were fascinated when they saw that all 3 sides were *exact whole numbers*. They came to be called *Pythagorean triplets*. In this activity you are going to make new discoveries about these triplets.

Part A

1. Andrea said that she found a Pythagorean triplet that had a side that measured *3 units* and a side that measured *4 units*.
   Is she correct? Justify your answer.
2. Mohammed then announced, "I can create other triplets from Andrea's set by just *multiplying each side by 2*."
   Is he correct? Justify your answer.
3. Musa said, "I can create other triples from Mohammed's idea." Mr. Samuel said, "That is great. Can you show me how you do it?"
   Your job is to determine what Musa did. Show your work and explain what you have done. In your explanation, discuss how many triples you can create using Mohammed's idea.
4. Anthony posed a problem for the class. "I found a triple whose *smallest side is 33*.
   Can you find the other sides?"

Part B: New Challenge

Monica was playing around with numbers and found one triple had a *hypotenuse* that measured *13 units*. It seemed very different from the triples we worked with up to now.
   Can you find if there is such a triple? Explain and show all your thinking.

Part C: Reflection

Write with as much detail as you can about all the new ideas you learned from doing this.

EXAMPLE 18: MOVING FROM ARITHMETIC TO ALGEBRA

Laws of Exponents: Generalizing Mathematical Ideas

Look at the following sets of powers. Find the solutions to each, changing all decimals to fractions. (*You can use a calculator.*)

2^5	5^5	10^5
2^4	5^4	10^4
2^3	5^3	10^3
2^2	5^2	10^2
2^1	5^1	10^1
2^0	5^0	10^0
2^{-1}	5^{-1}	10^{-1}
2^{-2}	5^{-2}	10^{-2}
2^{-3}	5^{-3}	10^{-3}
2^{-4}	5^{-4}	10^{-4}
2^{-5}	5^{-5}	10^{-5}

Now observe your results, looking for the different patterns.

What patterns do you see?

What questions do you have?

Are there any conjectures you can you make?

How can you prove if your conjectures will hold true for all cases?

EXAMPLE 19: MOVING FROM ARITHMETIC TO ALGEBRA

Working with Variables

What is the difference between **x + x and x * x** ?

Explain to the best of your ability. To answer this question, try to use real numbers in place of the variables to help in your explanation.

Now look at this pattern and come up with an explanation about adding radicals. Place these on the calculator and observe the results

$\sqrt{3} +$	$\sqrt{3} =$	$2\sqrt{3} =$
$3\sqrt{2} +$	$5\sqrt{2} =$	$8\sqrt{2} =$
$-4\sqrt{5} +$	$2\sqrt{5} =$	$-2\sqrt{5} =$

What observations can you make?

Make a conjecture about adding radicals.

Create another problem to test your conjecture.

Do you think this will always work? Why? Explain as fully as you can.

What connections do you see between **x + x** and $\sqrt{x} + \sqrt{x}$?

Based on your understanding of **x * x**, what do you think will happen when you multiply $\sqrt{x} * \sqrt{x}$?

To help you think about it, try $\sqrt{3} * \sqrt{3}$ and $\sqrt{5} * \sqrt{5}$

EXAMPLE 20: USE OF PHYSICAL STRUCTURES

Models of the Seagram Building

You will be given several photographic images of the Seagram Building, one of the important buildings in the history of American architecture and skyscraper history.

Using the drawings as best you can, and knowing that the height of the building is 525 feet, estimate/calculate the width and depth of the building. (It is very hard to be exact here.)

Now join with a partner and build a model of the building using your best guess for the width and depth of the building to the scale you pick out of a hat.

Once all the models are completed, they will be lined up in "size places."

In your groups:

- Record the patterns you observe with the models set in size places.
- Propose an alternate arrangement of the models. What pattern(s) might be observable then?
- Were all the buildings built in proportion? How can you prove this?

EXAMPLE 21: USE OF PHYSICAL STRUCTURES

How Tall Is Your School Building?

What do you estimate the length of the classroom to be?

How did you come up with your estimate?

What do you estimate the height of the room to be? Describe the method you used to find your answer.

(Now you will go outside to the front of the school.)

THE CHALLENGE:
A. Estimate the height of your school without any measuring tools. Explain how you determined your estimate.

B. Now you're going to be given a set of tools: a tape measure, a calculator, and an inclinometer. Your job is to use these tools to figure out the height of the building as accurately as you can. Show all the work and thinking your group did.

EXAMPLE 22: MODELING REAL-WORLD SITUATIONS

Model Suspension Bridge Project

You are an engineer for the City of New York and charged with designing and building a scale model of a suspension bridge. You will be given the length of a waterway that will be crossed by your bridge. Everyone will be given a different length. You will also be given a set of rules of thumb (at the end of the task) to help you make different decisions. Your task is:

1. Tower Placement/Span Length

Using the Rules of Thumb, decide where to put your towers in your waterway. How far from the land on either side do you want the towers to be? To do that, you need to figure out the length of both the main span and the side spans.

Next, decide how wide the towers should be. Show your calculations and sketch the waterway and towers.

2. The Roadway

Using the Rules of Thumb decide how high above the water your roadway will be.

Some questions to think about:

What is the purpose of your bridge?
Where it is located? Will ships be passing underneath?
Is the height of the water affected by tides? (For reference, the Verrazano
  Narrows Bridge has a height above water of around 216 feet.)
Show all of your calculations below.

3. Tower Height

Calculate how tall the towers must be above the roadway. Show all of your calculations below.

4. Quadratic Equation

Follow the steps below to find three points, which you will then use to find the equation of the main cable.

Sketch your bridge below and label it as follows:

- The roadway represents the x axis. Label the x axis.
- The **right side of the left tower** represents the y axis. Label the y axis.
- The point where the roadway meets the right side of the left tower is (0,0). Label this point.
- The height of your left tower represents the y intercept, because that is where the cable will be attached. Mark this point.
- The center of your cable at its lowest point should be in the middle of your roadway. **Use the Rules of Thumb to help you find that point**. Find the coordinates of this point and label it on your sketch.
- Find the coordinates of the point represented by the main cable meeting the **left side of the right tower**. Label this point.
- You can now use these three points to find the quadratic equation of the main cable. Write this equation below.

5: Vertical Suspenders

An important part of any suspension bridge is the placement of the vertical suspenders, which hold up the roadway. They must be equally spaced throughout your span, and symmetrical on either side of the vertex. How far apart are the suspender cables? (Use the information you gathered at the George Washington Bridge.) How many suspenders will you need for your bridge?

You need to only give 11 points on your main cable that has a suspender.

List the x-coordinates for these 11 points.

6: Vertical Suspenders Meet Main Cable

Knowing the equation of your parabolic main cable, and the x coordinates of the vertical suspenders, figure out the y coordinate where each of the 11 suspenders meets the main cable. Write these as ordered pairs and show all of your work below. Using the sketch you made in step 4, draw all of your vertical suspenders and mark the points where they meet the main cable.

7: Anchorages

A suspension bridge's anchorages are typically found on either side of the waterway the bridge spans. Decide how far from each tower the anchorages will be placed. The suspension cables that connect to the anchorages from the towers can be assumed to have a linear shape. To find the equation of each cable, follow the steps below:

• First, determine the coordinates of the point where the cable connects to the tower.
• Next, using your work from above, determine the coordinates of the inner edge of the anchorage.
• Use these points and the calculator to find the equation of the line (linear regression).

8: Architectural Design on a Coordinate Plane

You will be using graph paper to create an accurate architectural drawing of your design. Your drawing must include the towers, the roadway, suspension cables, vertical suspenders, and anchorages. All points previously discussed must be accurately labeled on your drawing. To begin, you must first decide on a scale based on the size of your bridge so that your drawing can fit on the graph paper (you may put four pieces of paper together). Show the calculations you used to determine your scale below.

Part II—Model Building

Your group will be constructing a model of the bridge you designed.

You are going to use your drawing to guide your work. That means you will use the same scale as you did in your architectural drawing.

In addition to the modeling, each group member will be required to complete one journal entry per class session describing the process of building the model. You may write about any aspect of the process, but it may help you to think about the following:

• What worked well for our group today?
• What challenges did our group face today? What can we do during the next class to overcome them?
• What did we accomplish today? What will we be working on during the next class?

Journal entries should be two to three paragraphs, and must be handed in after each class.

Rules of Thumb

These sets of measurements were created by engineers to give estimates of various relationships of different parts of a suspension bridge. You should use these ratios to help you make decisions as you design your suspension bridge.

LMS = Length of Main Span
LSS = Length of Side Span
SM = Sag of Main Span Cable from Top of Tower

- **Sag Ratio (SR) = SM/LMS = 1/12 to 1/9**
- **Span Length Ratio (SLR) = LSS/LMS = 1/6 to 1/2**
- **Total Height of Tower (HT) = LMS/7 to LMS/5**
- **Height of Tower above Roadway (HTA) = 0.60*HT to 0.65*HT**
- **Height of Tower below Roadway (HTB) = 0.40*HT to 0.35*HT**

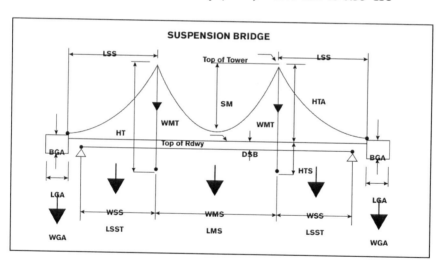

EXAMPLE 23: MODELING REAL-WORLD SITUATIONS

Shoe Size Problem

Shaquille O'Neal is 7 feet, 1 inch tall and has a 15-inch foot.
What do you think his shoe size is?

How did you come up with your prediction?

Now here is some information to see if your prediction is correct:
   The size of a shoe a person needs varies linearly with the length of his or her foot.
   You are going to gather data from at least five boys in the class to find out their shoe size and the length of their foot. Shaquille O'Neal has a 15-inch foot.

Describe the method you used to find the shoe size for all men.

Was your prediction correct?

Can you use your method to estimate the length of a man's foot who wears size 14 shoe?

Does a woman's shoe size follow the same pattern? Can you test it out with some girls in your class? Use your results to come up with a way of finding a woman's shoe size once you know the length of her foot.

EXAMPLE 24: USING GAMES TO UNDERSTAND MATHEMATICS

The Red and Yellow Swap

Directions

- Players take turns moving one chip at a time.
- A chip can only move forward (not backward).
- A chip can move into an empty square OR jump over a chip of the other color.
- A chip may not jump over a same-colored chip.

Starting Board

Y	Y	Y	Y	Y		R	R	R	R	R

Ending Board

R	R	R	R	R		Y	Y	Y	Y	Y

Your Task: Determine the least number of moves it will take for the red and yellow chips to switch places on the game board. Can you generalize this for any number of chips?

EXAMPLE 25: MODELING USING REAL-WORLD DATA

Concentration of Medication in a Patient's Blood over Time

The table below displays real data that shows what happens in your bloodstream when you take medication. Create at least two other representations that will help us understand the situation with greater clarity and depth. What representations did you choose? Why did you choose them? What connections can you make between the different representations? Which representation helps to make the data most understandable? Why?

Time (hours)	Concentration (milligrams per liter)
0.0	0.0
0.5	78.1
1.0	99.8
1.5	84.4
2.0	50.1
2.5	15.6

EXAMPLE 26: MODELING MATHEMATICAL IDEAS AND REAL-WORLD SITUATIONS

What Is Normal?

Today you are going to do an investigation and use the data you collect to develop an important concept in statistics.

You are going to flip 10 pennies 20 times. Each time you flip keep a record of how many heads there were. Once you have done it 20 times, collect the data from your classmates so you will have a large amount of tosses to work with.

Use the following table to organize your data. (Use the binomial theorem when working with the expected probabilities.)

Number of Heads	Expected Probability as Fraction and Percent	Actual Results as Fraction and Percent
0		
1		
2		
3		
4		
5		
6		
7		
8		
9		
10		

Create two frequency bar graphs; one for the expected probabilities and the other for the actual probabilities. Graph paper is available at the end of this task.

What do you observe about the data and the two frequency bar graphs?

Now mark a point at the midpoint of the top of each bar. Connect the data points with a smooth curve. What do you observe about the graphs? (Include shape, symmetry mean media, and mode in your discussion.)

What conclusions can you make about the theoretical representations and the representations with the actual data in relation to the normal curve? Is the theoretical distribution a good description of the actual event of flipping ten coins? Why?

Which of the following would you describe as normal? Explain using a graph. (You can go on the computer to collect data if you need to.)

1. The type of footwear students wear to school.
2. Family income in the United States.
3. The number of people in New York divided up by age group.
4. Heights of students in your class.

EXAMPLE 27: MATHEMATICAL MODELING

Can You Build the Most Efficient Container?

Challenge

You are a member of the engineering team at P&G Popcorn. This company believes in giving their customers more popcorn than any of their competitors. The company needs to design a popcorn-shipping container that will hold the maximum amount of popcorn. Your job is to design and build the container based on your knowledge of three-dimensional figures. Your container must be able to be closed on all sides, that is, it must have a top. Brainstorm different ideas with your team before you start to build. Write it down on paper and be ready to present why you think your design would be most efficient. We will test each of the containers to see which design holds the most popcorn based on the surface area of your design.

Materials

• One piece of construction paper
• Scissors
• Ruler
• Tape for edges only

EXAMPLE 28: MATHEMATICAL MODELING

Salary Choice

It is summer vacation and I'm bored to death. "I need a job," I think to myself. I find an ad for a job that mainly entails sitting in an office all day doing nothing. I wonder, "What is this?"

Two days later I go on the interview. The boss says little about the job except that I have a choice for my salary.

Here are the two options:

1. You earn 1 cent on the first day, 2 cents on the second day, and double your salary every day thereafter for the 30 days; or
2. Exactly $1,000 a day. (That's $30,000!)

I jump up out of my seat at that. "You've got your man. I'll take the $30,000," I yell.

What would you have done in this situation? Show all your work and give evidence for your decision.

EXAMPLE 29: LEARNING TO ABSTRACT: MOVING FROM ARITHMETIC TO ALGEBRA

The Square Border Problem

Opening Activity

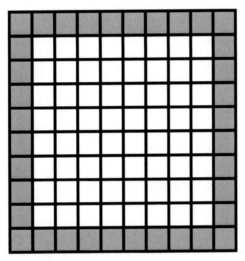

How many squares are in the blue border around the 10-by-10 grid on the right?

Write down the method you used to figure out how many blue border squares there are.

Make a numerical representation of your method.

Activity 2

Choose one of these methods and describe it below so that someone who wasn't in class would have a way to find the answer. Explain why the method works.

$10 + 9 + 9 + 8 = 36$
$10 * 4 - 4 = 36$
$10 + 10 + 8 + 8 = 36$

9 * 4 = 36
100 − 64 = 36
8 * 4 + 4 = 36

Activity 3

Now let us look at the patterns in another way:
   Here are five of the methods we discussed in class. Complete the chart leading to the generalization of each method (s represents the number of squares on each side).

Method for 10 by 10	9 by 9	8 by 8	7 by 7	s by s
10 + 9 + 9 + 8				
10 * 4 − 4				
10 + 10 + 8 + 8				
100 - 64				
8 * 4 + 4				

So there were multiple ways to solve this problem. What do you think will happen when you simplify each of the generalized expressions?

Now simplify each expression. What happened? Why did it happen?

Journal Writing: Write about what you have learned from today's experience with the Square Border Problem. Why do you think I wanted you to do this lesson?

EXAMPLE 30: ENCOURAGING THE USE OF EVIDENCE AND PROOF IN DAILY PROBLEM SOLVING

The Magical Exterior Angles

You now are going to try to discover an idea about the sum of the exterior angles of any regular polygon. Using the figures below, complete the following chart:

Number of Sides	Sum of the Exterior Angles
3	
4	

5	
6	
n	

1. Write a general statement about the sum of the exterior angles for any regular polygon.

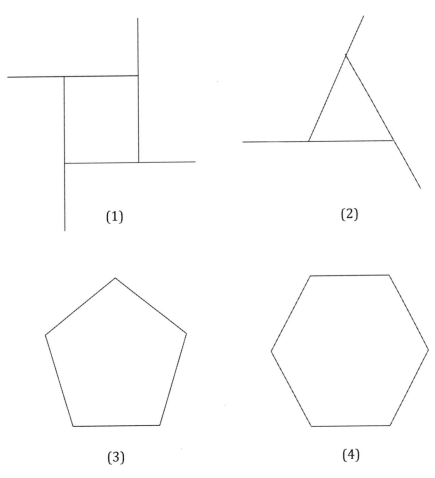

(1)   (2)

(3)   (4)

2. Do you think that the general statement you wrote for the sum of the exterior angles of a regular polygon would also work for any polygon, regular or not? WHY?

3. Test your theory by drawing a polygon below that is not regular. Extend the sides to form exterior angles and measure them. Did your theory hold true? How can you prove this idea using the drawings of any polygon?

Activity 2

1. We just looked at the Exterior Angle Sum Conjecture. Now you will look at it in a different way.
2. Draw a polygon of any size and its exterior angles. Label the exterior angles. Cut out the exterior angles and arrange them all about a point. Repeat this with another polygon with a different number of sides. Explain how this activity explains the Exterior Angle Sum Conjecture.
3. Now that you've made this new observation, why do you think this is happening?

EXAMPLE 31: PROJECTS OF THE WORLD THAT USE RICH MATHEMATICS

Creating a Fair Game

Here is your opportunity to become the creator of an exciting new game. It should be a game people would want to play and also mathematically rich. Your written piece should be broken up into 3 parts. The 3 parts are: **game description and instructions, explanation of probability,** and **fairness of game.**

Before you begin your work please look at the model project. It is there to spark your imagination, not to be replicated.

1. **Game Description and Instructions:** In this section you will give a detailed description of the game including all the necessary rules and instructions, describing how a person wins the game. You should describe what materials are needed to play the game.
2. **Explanation of Probability:** This is the most important section. You need to show through using the various probability concepts we learned how you came up with your game. You should include wherever possible the counting principle, permutation, combination, simple probability, compound probability, showing all possible outcomes using a sample space and tree diagram.
3. **Is the game fair?** In this section you need to answer the question posed by explaining how the rules you created are based on the probability of the

events. For example, if one outcome is 3 times harder to get than a second outcome then a rule involved with those 2 outcomes will reflect that idea.

The Coin Game

Game Description

The Coin Game can be played by two or more players. Each player is given **three pennies** and a **little man**. Each player places their **little man** at **GO**. The goal of the game is to be the first player to move around the board and reach **END.**

How do you play the game?

- Each player picks a token that he/she will move around the board.
- Each player flips his/her coins. The person with the most heads goes first.
- Player 1 takes his/her three coins and has to predict how the coins will land before he/she throws the coins.
- Player 1 flips the coins and counts the number of heads and tails.
- Use the following chart to determine the movement of your token around the board.

Number of Tails	Number of Heads	Prediction Is Correct	Prediction Is Wrong
3	0	6 steps forward	1 step back
2	1	2 steps forward	2 steps back
1	2	2 steps forward	2 steps back
0	3	6 steps forward	1 step back

- When you land on **?** you must answer one of the questions from the deck of questions. Another player reads the question. The answer is at the bottom of the card. If you are wrong you go to **Tutoring**.
- To get out of **Tutoring** you must answer a question or flip three tails. If you are unsuccessful you lose a turn.
- You cannot move backwards from **Start.**
- Every player gets one turn then the next player goes. After player 1 gets his/her turn player 2 goes.
- The first player to reach **Finish** wins the game.

Explanation of Probability

This game uses 3 coins. Each coin has 2 possible outcomes; head or tail. If you flip 3 coins there are going to be **8 possible outcomes**. Why?

Using the **counting principle** we know that there are 2 possible outcomes on each coin. We multiply the possible outcomes on each coin and we get 2*2*2 or **8 possible outcomes**. Let me prove it to you using a sample space.
Here is the sample space showing eight possible outcomes:

HHH
HHT
HTH
HTT
THH
THT
TTH
TTT

Here is a chart showing the probability of the different outcomes:

Number of Tails	Number of Heads	Probability
3	0	1/8
2	1	3/8
1	2	3/8
0	3	1/8

You should notice that the probabilities add up to 8/8 or 1 whole. This will always be true when you are up all the probabilities of an experiment.

When you look at the chart you will notice that it is three times more likely to get a head and 2 tails or a tail and 2 heads than getting 3 heads or 3 tails. This fact is reflected in the rules of the game. Notice that if you predict getting 3 heads or 3 tails and this event occurs then you move 6 places forward. If you predict 2 heads and a tail or 2 tails and a head and this event occurs you only move 2 places forward.
The questions on the cards in the deck are all questions from probability covering all the topics we studied.

For example:
How many 3-person groups can you form from 5 people?
Answer: $_5C_3$ or 10 different groups.

Is the Game Fair?

The game is definitely fair. It doesn't favor the person who predicts the less likely probability or the person who predicts the more likely probability. We can see that in the following statements.

If you predict 3 heads with a probability of 1/8, you move forward 6 places if you are correct and move back 1 place if you are wrong.

If you predict 2 heads and 1 tail with a probability of 3/8, you move forward 2 places if you are correct and move back 2 places if you are wrong.

Will the person who goes for the long shot or the person who goes for the sure thing win? It is hard to tell. That is why the game is fair.

Tutoring	?					
						?
Start / Finish			?			

Chapter Four

Guides for Teachers

GUIDES TO WRITE AND CRITIQUE LESSONS, UNITS, AND PERFORMANCE TASKS

Protocols and Tools for Self Evaluation, Reflection, and Goal Setting

The basic idea is that we professional educators should take charge of our own learning.

— McDonald, Dichter, and McDonald (2003)

How do you own what you teach? How do you see teaching as a creative experience? In this chapter, I share with you guides that will help you take charge of your learning. The documents in this chapter include guides to write lessons, units, and tasks to help you make teaching truly your own. I share with you protocols to help you deepen your understanding of teaching and learning. And share with you tools of reflection to help you and your colleagues think about what is happening in your classroom and the classrooms in your school. Here is a description of these guides and tools.

Questions to Think about When Planning an Inquiry-Based, Common-Core-Aligned Unit

This set of questions is organized into four parts: Big Ideas and Essential Questions, Common Core Standards, Development of Content, Concepts and Procedures, Assessments. Writing a unit is complex. While teachers can write a unit by themselves I recommend teachers use this tool in collaboration to create a meaningful rich unit. This tool does not stand alone. From working with this set of questions you can create an outline for a unit. The tools for developing the lessons and tasks that will be embedded in this unit are also in this chapter.

Guide to Writing an Inquiry Lesson and Inquiry-Based Lesson-Planning Template

The guide contains questions to help you formulate a lesson around a concept, procedure, problem, or combination of these. Many of the examples in the previous chapter arose from answering these types of questions.

The template is aligned to the guide with a structure to help set up inquiry activities leading to student mathematical understanding. Please be sure to read the opening Guiding Ideas and Questions before working with the template. Templates at first can often be overwhelming, so select the most important parts for you right now and grow toward using the rest of the template. The goal of providing this template is not to fill it out, but to help you create a coherent mathematical experience for your students. The template is not the end but a starting point of creating exciting experiences for your students.

List of Questions to Think about When Writing a Mathematical Performance Task

Performance tasks have been and are being defined in many different ways. When I talk about performance tasks I am referring to tasks that have open-endedness to the questions. This leads to student work that looks different in its problem-solving approach, reasoning, communication, representations, and connections. This means that the performance task is focused on students using their mathematical understandings rather than replicating a learned procedure. These tasks can be a ten-minute opening to a lesson, a full period where students are working in groups or independently, or it could be done over a longer period of time.

This tool can be used to think deeply about the creation of a rigorous task that engages students in rich mathematics. This work becomes very important with the new Common Core State Standards and the use of performance tasks as a means of assessing student mathematical understanding. This tool should be used in conjunction with the Questions to Think about When Planning an Inquiry-Based, Common-Core-Aligned Unit.

Big Ideas in Various Areas of Mathematics

This is a set of documents to help teachers think about the big ideas and underlying structures within mathematics. The writers of the Common Core Standards of Practice state that, "Mathematically proficient students look closely to discern a pattern or structure" (p. 8). This is one of the big ideas inherent to all branches of mathematics. Helping students think about the big ideas will help them begin to discern the structures within mathematics. The big idea of *doing and undoing* in algebra (Driscoll 1999) or the idea that *measurement is relative* (Lockhart 2012) are two examples of those powerful structures.

Teachers should use these documents when creating lessons and units to help think about this question, "What do I want my students to think about in today's lesson or upcoming unit?"

Questions for Students to Ask Themselves When Solving a Problem

This set of questions should be shared with students early in the school year as a tool to help them become flexible and strategic problem solvers. Good problem solvers learn how to ask themselves questions and are willing to rethink the chosen strategy in the middle of the process. This document will help in developing that ability.

An Inquiry Approach to Look at Student Work and Performance Tasks/Lessons/Activities

These are two protocols whose purpose is to help teachers look deeply at their craft. In effective protocols, teachers gather together to look closely at tasks and/or student work and act as critical friends to help their colleagues deepen their thinking about good instruction. These protocols are described as inquiry protocols because the presenter always begins with a question that he/she would like to be at the center of the discussion.

Teacher's Perceptions Continuum and Student's Perceptions Continuum

These were created to help teachers reflect on their craft in terms of pedagogy and the learning of mathematics. Teachers can use the Teacher's Perception Continuum to analyze where they are currently as math teachers and where they hope to be in the coming months. The Student's Perception Continuum gives teachers important information so they can learn how students perceive their experience in the mathematics classroom.

School Mathematics: A Self-Assessment

This is a document that was created for a school's team of math teachers to assess where the school/math department stands in the ongoing process of developing a program that successfully prepares students to think mathematically and to be college ready. This document is based on A Vision of an Inquiry-Based Mathematics Classroom, featured in chapter 1. This tool can be used at different points in the school year to assess the development of the mathematics program in a school.

Guide to Creating a Vision and Four-Year Plan

It is crucial that a math team at a school have a coherent four-year plan that will support the development of mathematical thinking and understanding. A math team at a school would need to come together over a period of time to collaborate on this process. This guide and the accompanying questions arise from A Vision of an Inquiry-based Mathematics Classroom.

QUESTIONS TO THINK ABOUT WHEN PLANNING AN INQUIRY-BASED, COMMON CORE UNIT

Big Ideas and Essential Questions

- What is the essence of the mathematics in this unit?
- What are the topics within this unit?
- What do I want my students to think about in this unit?
- What are the big ideas in the unit?
- Why do I want students to think about these big ideas?
- Can I create an essential question(s) for this unit built around these big ideas?
- How will this unit engage students to think about an idea(s) and encourage them to raise questions?
- What are the enduring understandings I want my students to be able to talk about five years from now?

Common Core Standards

- What are the content standards I want to teach in this unit?
- How do I intend to incorporate the Standards of Practice and ideas of inquiry instruction in the unit?
  - Problem solving
  - Quantitative and abstract reasoning
  - Mathematical modeling
  - Developing an understanding of the underlying structures in mathematics

Development of Content: Concepts and Procedures

- What are the different concepts and procedures I want my students to think about and engage in within this unit?
- How do I see the relationship between the concepts and procedures being taught? How do I ensure that students see these relationships?
- How can I set up different situations (e.g., investigations, performance tasks) so my students can begin to make sense of the different concepts and procedures?
- Are there any tools/manipulatives/models I can use in lessons within the unit to help students to think about an idea in different ways?

- How are my lessons going to be developed so students see the connectedness between the different lessons?

Assessments

- How will I know what my students really understand about the big ideas and their accompanying concepts and procedures?
- How do I intend to embed performance tasks within the unit?
- Is there a product students have to produce at the end of a unit that shows their understanding?

LIST OF QUESTIONS TO THINK ABOUT WHEN WRITING A MATHEMATICAL PERFORMANCE TASK

- What topic(s) from your unit do you want to embed within the task? Why should students learn these topics?
- What are the big ideas from your unit that you want your students to think about within the task?
- What knowledge do you want students to present and/or what new knowledge do you want them to be able to construct through the performance assessment experience?
- What do you want to assess in this task? (e.g., problem-solving strategies, flexibility with procedure, conceptual understanding)
- What do you want to learn about your students' mathematical thinking and understanding from this task?
- What is the context for the task? Why would that context engage students?
- What are you going to ask students to do? Why do you want them to do it?

Once you have a first draft . . .

- Does the task ask students to think and wonder about mathematical ideas?
- Is the task sufficiently open-ended so there will be diversity of product?
- Will students with different levels of math ability be able to enter into this task and find it both interesting and challenging?
- Will this task give you the information you want to find out?
- Do you expect students to communicate their mathematical thinking and their process, which might also include rethinking of strategy?

GUIDE TO WRITING AN INQUIRY LESSON

1. What do I want my students to understand at the end of the lesson?
   a. Concept
   b. Procedure

  c. The relationship between the concept and procedure

  d. A problem-solving strategy

2. What would it mean for a student to understand this?

3. Why do I want my students to know this?

4. Can I create a situation/activity that will help students discover the desired concept and/or procedure or develop an understanding of the problem-solving strategy?

5. Will this be a bare number problem or will it be augmented by a contextual situation?

6. Will students find the activity interesting? Challenging? Why?

7. How can I differentiate it so that all students can participate in the activity?

8. Does this activity ask groups of students to

  a. Make observations?

  b. Raise questions?

  c. Gather data?

  d. Look for patterns?

  e. Make conjectures and generalizations?

9. Does my activity encourage discussion, argument, defending of ideas?

10. How will I know that my students understand the concepts and/or procedure?

11. What Common Core Practice standards is this lesson aligned to?

12. What Common Core Content standards is this aligned to?

INQUIRY-BASED LESSON PLANNING TEMPLATE

A set of ideas and questions are presented before you begin to write the lesson. The purpose is to help you think about the lesson with both nuance and depth.

On Learning

Since we are developing conceptual understanding and procedural fluency, it is important to think about what it means to understand the ideas and procedures that will be embedded in the lesson.

  Learning is fluid and ongoing. It's not expected that mastery be accomplished at the end of one period. How are you going to gauge your students' movement along the continuum of understanding of the ideas and procedures? When in the progression of the lesson do you want to check on their thinking?

On Planning

The lesson plan articulates our intentions and a pathway through the lesson, but the journey through it is flexible. Every lesson will not require an opening, two subsequent activities, and a closing as is currently outlined in the template. The point is to be thoughtful about what are the experiences your students need to make sense of the mathematics.

Another important idea is that if we want the lesson to be student centered then student questions and ideas need inform the direction of the lesson. So a lesson can be redirected by students' questions or misconceptions. How do I prepare for this?

Before you write the lesson take time to think about the misconceptions and missing conceptions your students might bring to the lesson.

A development of a concept or procedure takes multiple experiences, so a lesson should not be seen as a one period necessarily.

Unit:	Lesson:		Date:
Unit Essential Question(s):	**Lesson Focus Question:**		
What do you hope students will be able to do and think about at the end of this lesson? (Your answer to this question should inform your plan for the lesson.)			
What connections to prior knowledge do you want students to make?	Materials needed?		

Standards Addressed:	What will students be doing and thinking about? (Include differentiation notes)	What will the teacher be doing? What misconceptions do you think will be encountered? What questions are you going to ask students?
Opening Activity *This can be a short problem, a puzzle, a provocative question, a standardized-test-type situation.* • *What do you hope to learn about student mathematical thinking from this activity?* • *How is this activity setting up the rest of the lesson?* • *What **misconceptions** might students express during this opening activity?*		

Standards Addressed:	**What will students be doing and thinking about?** (Include differentiation notes)	**What will the teacher be doing?** What misconceptions do you think will be encountered? What questions are you going to ask students?
Second Activity *This could be an investigation, the development of procedural, or conceptual understanding, and development of a problem-solving strategy.*		

	What will students be doing and thinking about? (Include differentiation notes)	**What will the teacher be doing?** What misconceptions do you think will be encountered? What questions are you going to ask students?
Third Activity *This should build off the Second Activity; it could be both practice and expanded ways to think about the ideas students grappled with in the Second Activity; this could be a formative assessment.*		
Closing Activity *Here you are going to assess student understanding of the ideas presented in today's class. It could be an exit problem, or journal writing.* ****Student understandings will vary from lesson to lesson, so you want to do your best to differentiate what meaning students made out of the lesson.**		

How will students be grouped?	Why will they be grouped this way?	Student Groupings

Reflections on the lesson:

QUESTIONS TO THINK ABOUT WHEN WRITING A MATHEMATICAL PERFORMANCE TASK

Before you write the performance task it is important that you think about the unit in which the task will be embedded. The questions below will be broken up in to two sections. In the first section you will be thinking about the unit and in the second section you will then focus on the task.

- Reflecting on the unit:
- What are your unit topic(s)?
- What are the big ideas in this unit?
- What are the mathematical/conceptual understandings you want your students to come away with from this unit?
- What are the skills/procedures that students will develop through this unit?
- What prior skills/understandings do you expect students to have coming into this unit?
- What misconceptions do you anticipate that students might have?

Reflecting on the performance task:

- What topic(s) from your unit do you want to embed within the task? Why should students learn these topics?
- What are the big ideas from your unit that you want your students to think about within the task?
- What new knowledge do you want them to be able to construct through the performance assessment experience?
- What do you want to assess in this task?
- What is the context for the task? Why would that context engage students?
- What are you going to ask students to do? Why do you want them to do it?
- What do you want to learn about your students' mathematical thinking and understanding from this task?
- Does the task ask students to think and wonder about mathematical ideas?
- Is the task sufficiently open-ended so there will be diversity of product?

- Will students with different levels of math ability be able to enter into this task and find it both interesting and challenging?
- Do you expect students to communicate their mathematical thinking and their process, which might also include rethinking of strategy?
- What Common Core Content standards is this aligned to?

BIG IDEAS IN ALGEBRA

Questions for teachers to think about:

- What is the essence of algebra?
- Why do mathematicians describe algebra as generalized arithmetic?

Questions to thinking about related to the teaching of algebra:

- Why should my students learn these ideas?
- What do I want my students to know and think about at the end of a unit and even five years from now?
- How are these different ideas connected?
- How can I help students make sense of these ideas?

Number Sense

How comfortable are my students with numbers?
Can they talk about the relation of whole numbers, integers, rational and irrational numbers?
Can they use a number line to talk about these sets of numbers?
Are they comfortable manipulating numbers?
Do they know why they do what they do?
How can I use problems to help students construct deeper understandings of basic arithmetic ideas?
How will I use students' number sense to develop algebraic ideas and procedures?
How can I help my students develop as estimaters?

Patterns/Pattern Recognition

Is mathematics the science of patterns?
Can the search for patterns help my students generalize algebraic ideas?

What is the relation between the concrete and the abstract, arithmetic and algebra?

How can the concrete help us understand the abstract?

How can the specific cases within arithmetic lead us to the general case as represented algebraically?

The Concept of Variable

Does the variable represent an unknown, one finite value, or an infinite amount of values?

How is the variable a pattern generalizer?

How does a variable differ in an algebraic expression, equation, and an inequality?

Is the variable the bridge between arithmetic and algebra?

Representation

How can I use visual representations to develop the understanding of algebraic concepts and procedures?

What is the relation between verbal, symbolic, and graphical representations?

Do my students see the relationship between table, equation, and graph within functions?

Procedural Fluency

What is the interrelationship between concept and procedure?

Why is that interrelationship essential for student understanding?

What does it mean for a student to be flexible with procedure?

How important is it for students to understand that there are multiple ways to work with algebraic expressions and relationships?

How can geometric representations be used for understanding algebraic procedures (e.g., the differences of two squares)?

Proportionality

What does proportional reasoning look like with and without specific numbers? How do I help students develop proportional reasoning?

How do we help students to move away from thinking just procedurally (e.g., cross-multiplication) about proportionality to the concept of proportionality?

How does proportionality help us understand a type of relationship?

How does it affect a student's understanding of linearity?

How is the concept of ratio a basis to understanding many different mathematical ideas (e.g., pi, sine, probability of an event, slope, and direct variation)?

Equality

What does the notion of equality mean?

Can their misconceptions cause my students difficulty in working with equalities?

Must the students understand the notion of equality or balance in order to manipulate equations?

Functions

How do functions help us understand and explain the world around us? How do my students compare linear, quadratic, and exponential functions?

Can they use tables, equations, and graphs to compare them?

What story do these different functions tell?

How can understanding functions help a person to make predictions?

How can I use real-world sets of data to help students understand the value and use of functions?

What if things in the world didn't behave like a function?

Doing and Undoing

How is doing and undoing central to many procedural and conceptual relationships in algebra?

How can we use the idea of doing and undoing to help students make sense of underlying structures of algebra?

Why does Paul Lockhart, a mathematician, describe algebra as the "tangling and untangling of numerical relationships" (2012, 56)?

Problem Solving

Is problem solving at the heart of mathematics?

How can my students learn to be metacognitive or think about their own thinking?

Can problems be used to develop mathematical concepts and procedures and not just be used as an application of learned concepts?

Why do mathematicians describe the solution to a problem as an argument rather than a number? What does this say about the teaching of algebra?

BIG IDEAS IN GEOMETRY

Questions for teachers to think about:

- What is the essence of geometry?
- How is geometry both of the imaginary world and the real world?

Questions to thinking about related to the teaching of geometry:

- Why should my students learn these ideas?
- What do I want my students to know and think about at the end of a unit and even five years from now?
- How are these different ideas connected?
- How can I help students make sense of these ideas?

Measurement

How is measurement a relative idea? How can we use this idea to compare different geometric representations?

How will a change in one measurement in a two- or three-dimensional figure affect the other measurements of that figure?

How can we maximize the ratio of area to perimeter in a two-dimensional figure or surface area to volume in a three-dimensional figure?

What is the relationship between line and angle in a two-dimensional plane figure?

How can I use the tools of measurement (protractor, ruler, compass, coordinate plane, etc.) to discover postulates and theorems of geometry?

How is perfection and imperfection present as we think about geometric ideas?

Patterns/Pattern Recognition

Is mathematics the science of patterns?

Can the search for patterns help my students generalize geometric ideas?

Do theorems come from generalizations?

Do patterns help us differentiate and distinguish between polygons (e.g., the sum of the angles of a polygon: internal, exterior, and central)?

What is the relationship between polygons and a circle?

How can I use analytic geometry to connect algebra and geometry, resulting in powerful methods of analysis and problem solving?

Transformations: Motion in Space

How can I help students understand congruence and similarity from the perspective of transformations?

How can I use rotation, reflection, translation, and dilation to understand the natural and manmade world?

Does the artists' use of transformations and geometric shapes have a place in the mathematics classroom?

Congruence and Similarity

Why is the notion of congruence an interesting idea?

How do you relate the notion of algebraic equality with geometric equality?

How can we use the understanding of transformations and rigid motion to develop an understanding of congruence?

How is the geometric notion of invariance and change essential to understanding similarity?

How are the ideas of congruence and similarity connected to the world we live in?"

Evidence and Proof

How do students use evidence to support their thinking in geometry?

Are more intuitive, visual ways of understanding geometric relationships a precursor to more formal explorations of geometric ideas? Can an informal sense of proof lead to more formal proof?

Why is it valuable for a student to study proof?

How can I give my students experience with analytic and deductive reasoning?

Why do mathematicians describe the solution to a problem as an argument rather than a number? What does this say about the teaching of geometry?

Problem Solving

Is problem solving at the heart of mathematics?

How can problem solving be used to help the traditional notion of abstract theorems come alive to students?

How can problem solving be used to understand the properties of geometric figures found in structures both natural and manmade? How can problem solving be used in geometry to help us understand the world we live in?

BIG IDEAS IN PROBABILITY AND STATISTICS

Questions for teachers to think about:

- What is the essence of probability?
- What is the essence of statistics?

Questions to thinking about related to the teaching of probability and statistics:

- Why should my students learn these ideas?
- What do I want my students to know and think about at the end of a unit and even five years from now?
- How are these different ideas connected?
- How can I help students make sense out of these ideas?

Creating, Describing, and Comparing Data

What story does this data tell me?
How can I represent this data?
What story does the visual graph tell me?
How can I use measures of central tendency to understand the data more deeply?
Why is mean associated with symmetric data?
Why is median associated with skewed data?
What can the shape and the spread of the data distribution tell me about the meaning of the data?
How can I use data to make inference and justify conclusions?
Why is randomness important in drawing statistical conclusions?
How can data be misused/abused? Why should a student care about this data?

Patterns

What are the patterns that I see in the different representations (e.g., graphs, numbers, and diagrams) of data?
What conjectures/hypotheses can I make?
How can I test my hypotheses/conjectures?

Statistical and Probabilistic Concepts and Procedures

How can I help my students develop the rules and formulas for probability from looking at the data in the sample space and tree diagrams?
What is the difference between AND and OR?

Can Venn diagrams help my students generalize ideas of mutually exclusive and overlapping events?

Can tree diagrams help my students generalize ideas of independent and dependent events?

How can I use patterns in data to develop the normal curve and the standard deviation?

Experimental versus Theoretical Probability

What is the relation between experimental and theoretical probability?

How can games help my students understand the concepts of probability?

How does an experiment with one trial compare with an experiment with 10,000 trials?

How does an understanding of ratio help my students understand probability?

Making Predictions or Probabilistic Reasoning

How can I help students use data to make sensible predictions and sensible decisions?

What predictions decisions can a student make from a scatter plot? Probability distribution?

How can I help students look at their misconceptions about probability?

Problem Solving

Is problem solving at the heart of mathematics?

How can my students learn to be metacognitive or think about their own thinking?

Can problems be used to develop mathematical understanding, not just an application of learned concepts?

How can I use real-world problems to develop ideas of counting (including permutations and combinations), independent and dependent events, correlation, regression, and line of best fit?

QUESTIONS FOR STUDENTS TO ASK THEMSELVES WHEN SOLVING A PROBLEM

- What is the problem about?
- What am I trying to find out?
- Does this problem remind me of other problems I have seen?

- What is my plan for solving the problem?
- What strategy might I use to begin to solve the problem?
- Are there any questions that I have that I might want to ask my classmates or teacher?
- Would simplifying the problem help me solve the problem? How would I do it?
- How can I use what I observed in the simpler problem and transfer that observation to the more complex problem?
- How can I organize the information in the problem?
- Can I create a set of data from the problem and look for a pattern?
- Can I make a conjecture from the observed pattern that I can test? Would this conjecture hold for all cases? How would I know?
- Could I use the pattern that I have observed and the conjecture that I have tested to answer the question? How would I do that?
- Do I need to rethink my strategy and attempt a different strategy? What might it be?
- Would drawing a diagram help me in any way?
- Could I work backward to help solve the problem?
- Can I attempt a graphical or algebraic approach? How would I do it?
- Once I have an answer, how do I know if the answer makes sense?
- Can I defend my process and solution to the rest of the class? What would I say?
- What did I learn from solving this problem? How can I use what I learned in further problem-solving situations?

AN INQUIRY APPROACH TO LOOKING AT STUDENT WORK

Teachers will have the opportunity to begin to develop a deeper understanding of their students' mathematical thinking by looking closely at their students' work on a teacher-created task or activity. The goal is to help teachers begin to answer their question(s) and support them with suggested teaching practices to help improve the students' mathematical thinking and understanding. Please use the note-taking document, found on pg. 111, to assist you in this process.

Each teacher will pose one question that he or she would like to discuss with the group based on his or her own inspection of the students' work. The teacher will share three representative pieces of student work for the group to examine and discuss. The teacher can/should use Indicators of Student Demonstration of Mathematical Thinking (see pg. 22) to help formulate his or her question.

Example Questions:

- What can I learn about my students' thinking from the strategies they chose?
- What can we observe about my students' reasoning skills?
- What can I learn about my students' ability to think algebraically?
- What can we observe about my students' ability to take a contextual situation and think about it mathematically?

Before you begin the process each participant should make sure they understand the task and its nuance by doing the task themselves.

Step 1

Teacher presents his or her question and gives an explanation of why this is an important question based on the student work (e.g., What can I learn about my students' thinking from the strategies they chose to solve the problem?). *(3 to 5 minutes)*

Step 2

Each member of the group looks closely at the student work and writes down his or her observations in relation to the question. The Indicators of Student Demonstration of Mathematical Thinking may/should be used to support observations (e.g., using the communication dimension in relation to student presentation of their thinking). *(5 to 7 minutes)*

Step 3

Observations are presented by each member of the group. Presenting teacher listens. Everyone takes notes about what is said. *(7 minutes)*

Step 4

Group members look closely at the notes to find connections and meaningful information that would be useful to the teacher. *(5 minutes)*

Step 5

Group members present their findings based on their analysis by asking questions and/or sharing ideas that would be useful to the presenting teacher. Presenting teacher listens. *(7–10 minutes)*

Step 6

Presenting teacher responds to feedback. Group members listen. *(3 minutes)*

Step 7

All discuss next steps. *(5 minutes)*

An Inquiry Approach to Looking at Student Work: Note-Taking Document

What is the question the presenter wants us to discuss?

Write down your observations from the student work that is related to the question.

Use the **Student Demonstration of Mathematical Thinking** to assist you. You are describing only what you see here, without analysis.

Take down notes about the observations made by all members of your group.

Based on your notes, what connections can you make or patterns can you find that would be meaningful for the presenter?

Questions you might ponder:

What patterns do you see in the data?
What do you think the patterns might mean?
What does it say about the students' mathematical thinking?

What next steps might the presenter take to help support his or her students? You can look at Indicators of Instructional Practices to help.

AN INQUIRY APPROACH TO LOOKING AT A TEACHER-CREATED TASK, ACTIVITY, OR LESSON

The goal is to help all participants to create a meaningful task, activity, or lesson in which they can learn about their students' mathematical thinking and understanding. Please use the note-taking document, found on pg. 113, to assist you in this process.

Step 1

Each presenter will discuss the task, activity, or lesson in relation to its purpose and what he or she hopes to learn about his or her student's mathematical thinking. The presenter might talk about the creation of the task based on the documents, How to Write an Inquiry Lesson or List of Questions to Think about When Writing a Mathematical Performance Task. The presenter will share how the task, activity, or lesson is aligned to the Common Core Standards. Finally, the presenter will share any concerns/questions he or she has about the task, activity, or lesson that his or her colleagues might help answer. *(5 to 7 minutes)*

Step 2

Each member of the group looks closely at the task, activity, or lesson and writes down his or her observations in relation to the teacher's presentation. If there are any clarifying questions, members of the group can share them at this time. *(5 minutes)*

Step 3

Each member of the group makes observations including responses to the presenter's questions/concerns. This is not the time to make recommendations but rather to share what you see. Presenting teacher listens without commenting. All take notes of what is said. *(7 to 10 minutes)*

Step 4

Presenter responds to observations. *(5 minutes)*

Step 5

The whole group makes recommendations to strengthen the task, activity, or lesson in terms of learning about students' development as mathematical thinkers. *(10 minutes)*

An Inquiry Approach to Looking at Teacher-Created Task, Activity, or Lesson: Note-Taking Document

What is the purpose of the task, activity, or lesson and the presenter's questions and/or concerns?

What are your observations of the task in relation to:

a. Teacher purpose.
b. What the teacher hoped students would learn from the experience.
c. Teacher concern/question.

What are the observations of the other participants?

What recommendations do you have for the presenter?

114

Teacher's Perceptions Continuum

Name: _____

Most of the time when I teach . . .

Concepts or Mathematical Ideas	. . . I explain concepts with students listening to what I say.	. . . I develop concepts with student assistance and my questioning.	. . . I place students in groups where they develop concepts with my assistance and support.	. . . I create contextual situations where groups of students make observations, collect data, look for patterns, conjecture, test out their ideas and then generalize concepts.
Rules and Formulas	. . . I give students rules and formulas and expect the students to memorize them.	. . . the rules and formulas are developed in class and I expect the students to memorize them.	. . . the students develop the rules and formulas with my assistance, which makes it easier for the students to remember them.	. . . the students will discover rules and formulas by using the process above. This process makes for greater potential of student understanding and remembering.
Procedures	. . . I model procedures and students practice them.	. . . I have students model procedures at the blackboard.	. . . I help students develop procedures from concepts.	. . . my students discover procedures from a developed understanding of a concept.

Problem Solving	. . . I use traditional word problems (e.g., consecutive integer problems) for applying a concept.	. . . I use traditional word problems and have students present them at the board.	. . . I use all types of problems, including nontraditional and real-world problems to help students develop greater strategic competence.	. . . I use all types of problems as my central tool for teaching to help students develop mathematical concepts, discover new ideas, and for greater strategic competence.
Questioning	. . . my questions primarily require factual recall.	. . . some of my questions are open-ended and they encourage different approaches to thinking.	. . . most of my questions are open-ended, encouraging different approaches to thinking, and are connected to a particular learning goal.	. . . my students generate questions that help guide the direction of the lesson.
Assignments	. . . my assignments typically require students to reproduce what they just learned.	. . . a few of my assignments ask students to discover ideas and show evidence to support their thinking.	. . . many of my assignments are structured so that students discover new ideas and provide evidence for their thinking.	. . . my assignments are based on students' questions and are structured so that students will discover new ideas that they can prove.
View of the Lesson	. . . I see each lesson as a discrete learning experience.	. . . I make connections between concepts taught in different lessons.	. . . I see different lessons as part of a unit with connections to a big idea.	. . . I create lessons as part of a unit that arises out of students' questions and interests about a big idea.

Assessment	. . . my assessments are mainly teacher-made tests or standardized exams.	. . . my assessments are mainly teacher-made tests with some use of authentic assessment.	. . . I use various types of authentic assessment along with teacher-made tests, including project-based assessments as a culmination of a math unit.	. . . I use various types of authentic assessment as my main mode of assessment. They arise from the inquiry experience and student-generated questions.

Student's Perceptions Continuum

How to complete this continuum: Look at each row separately. Read each statement always beginning with the words, "When I am in the math class." Then circle the square that best represents who you are. You can circle separate sentences in a square if the whole box doesn't represent who you are. It is important that you try to be as truthful as possible.

Most of the time when I am in math class . . .

Productive Disposition	. . . I feel **confused.** Very little of what goes on makes sense to me.	. . . I feel **OK.** Even though I don't understand much of what is said, I can follow what to do and get the right answer.	. . . I feel **good.** Math is interesting. It makes a lot of sense. I enjoy trying to figure things out.	. . . I feel really **good.** I love the challenge of mathematics, figuring out new things, discovering new ideas, seeing the connection between different ideas.
Concepts or Mathematical Ideas	. . . I don't **understand what the ideas being talked about mean.** When I want to, I write the idea down in my notebook and I might try to memorize it.	. . . I listen as **the teacher explains ideas but often don't understand what is being explained.** If I am able to follow what the teacher says, I will try to practice doing math examples.	. . . I **understand many ideas discussed in the class.** I can begin to talk about the idea and its relation to other ideas.	. . . I **understand most ideas.** I've thought about them and why they are true. I can discuss an idea and its relation to other ideas. I can explain an idea clearly to others.
Rules and Formulas	. . . I might **memorize rules and formulas** and attempt to apply them in examples similar to the	. . . I **memorize the rules and formulas that the teacher develops in class** and I will attempt	. . . I often **understand the meaning of different rules and formulas.** I can use the formula/rule	. . . I **understand most rules and formulas and why they make sense.** I can talk about the meaning of

	ones the teacher modeled in the class.	to apply them in various examples to make sure I can do it.	with some flexibility.	the formula/rule and use it in a variety of problems.
Procedures	**. . . I sometimes follow the model example of doing procedures** and might be able to repeat it in practice.	**. . . I can imitate the rules for procedures and do similar problems,** explaining the steps I followed. It is like following a cookbook recipe.	**. . . I understand why the procedure makes sense and its connection to an idea.** I can use it in various problems, not just the one the teacher did on the board.	**. . . I am often able to discover/create a procedure from understanding an idea. I** can use this procedure with all types of problems.
Problem Solving	**. . . I have difficulty solving word problems. I** try to follow the steps my teacher wrote on the board.	**. . . I can solve many word problems from the textbook,** explaining the procedures I followed.	**. . . I can solve different types of problems, including unusual ones and real-world problems** because I have had many opportunities to do this in the class.	**. . . I can solve all types of problems in order to develop and discover mathematical ideas and apply these ideas.** I use different strategies because problems are used every day in the classroom.
Questioning	**. . . I don't like to ask or answer questions in the class** because I feel unsure of myself.	**. . . I like to answer some questions and ask questions of the teacher** so he or she can give me the answer.	**. . . I like to answer questions that are open-ended and think about different ideas. I** ask	**. . . I like to ask meaningful questions and work to find out the answers. I** like to argue about ideas and

			questions when I need help analyzing ideas and problems.	defend my thinking with evidence. I look to the teacher to help guide me in my thinking.
Assignments	**. . . I do few assignments.** Those that I feel comfortable doing typically require me to imitate what I just learned.	**. . . I do many of my assignments.** I am most comfortable doing exercises in the textbook and feel unsure of myself when I have to solve problems or figure things out on my own.	**. . . I like to do assignments in which I have to discover new ideas** and provide evidence for my thinking. It can be very challenging but satisfying when I can make new discoveries.	**. . . I like to do assignments that arise from the questions of students in my class.** I like assignments that ask me to be creative with mathematics and make me think about ideas more deeply.
View Lessons	**. . . I see each lesson as separate from each other.** I rarely see any connection between what I learn in one lesson and another lesson a week later.	**. . . I see some connections between ideas taught in different lessons.** When I see connections I feel better about math.	**. . . I often see different lessons as part of a unit with the ideas and procedures connected to each other.** This helps me to see math as making sense.	**. . . I see different lessons as part of a unit with the concepts and procedures connected to a big idea.** This helps me to see math as a logical body of knowledge.
Working with Others	**. . . I prefer to work by myself** because I don't	**. . . it sometimes helps me to understand**	**. . . it often helps me to understand by talking**	**. . . discussing mathematical ideas and solving**

	improve my understanding by working with others.	**things when I talk with others** about what I am learning.	**with others** and making sense of math ideas and solving problems.	**problems with other students helps me to think more clearly and deeply.**
Assessment	**. . . I hate assessments.** Tests make me uncomfortable. When I try to study I feel it is a waste of time trying to memorize rules and formulas.	**. . . I am most comfortable with assessments in which I have to replicate what the teacher taught** us. I don't like questions that force me to think or ones we never learned.	**. . . I like to do different kinds of assessments; tests, class activities, and projects.** I like to show what I understand.	**. . . I like assessments that ask us to be creative.** I want my ideas and questions to be part of the assessment. I want to use what I understand to understand new things.
Overall Attitude	**. . . I don't really care because it has nothing to do with my life.**	**. . . I want to be able to understand, but this happens only sometimes.**	**. . . I often understand because math usually makes sense.**	**. . . I usually understand what is going on and I want to keep on learning new things.**

School Mathematics Self-Assessment

Directions: Teachers will rate their school and their students from 1 to 5 (with 1 representing lowest and 5 highest in college readiness.)

I. Student Mathematical Proficiency

Our students are able to:	1–5
talk deeply about the meaning of mathematical concepts	
see the connections and interrelationships between mathematical concepts	
see the relationship between mathematical concepts and procedures	
speak about what a procedure means and why it makes sense	
grapple with all types of mathematical problems	
use multiple strategies to solve all types of problems	
defend their process and answer with explanation, justification, and proof	
critique the reasoning of others and refine their own reasoning based on others' feedback	
reflect on their thinking and learning as a means of self-evaluation and growth as a learner	

II. What does instruction look like in our school?

The teacher gives students multiple opportunities to:	1–5
tackle open-ended challenging problems and help them develop strategies and various ways of thinking and approaching the problem	
construct new knowledge through investigations using interesting tasks and activities	
become pattern hunters and see the importance of patterns as a means of generalizing mathematical ideas	
share their conjectures, ideas, and solutions	
argue about mathematics and defend their ideas with evidence and proof	
ask questions and work to answer them with the teacher acting as the guide for the students	
think both algebraically and geometrically	
see that mathematics learning takes place both inside the classroom and outside in the world	
see that mathematics learning is a collaborative endeavor.	

III. How do students view mathematics at our school?

Our students view mathematics as:	1–5
making sense and having a coherent structure	
a means of solving problems	
an interesting subject worth the time and challenge to wonder about	
deeply connected through big ideas	
an interrelationship between concept and procedure	
meaningful for their lives.	

Our students view themselves as being:	1–5
capable of doing mathematics	
capable of thinking and reasoning mathematically	
capable of solving different types of problems and willing to struggle and persevere.	

GUIDE TO CREATING A VISION AND FOUR-YEAR PLAN

It's important to develop a four-year plan for mathematics to ensure that students have the opportunity to experience a rich, demanding, and exciting mathematics education that prepares them well for college. The work begins with the team of mathematics teachers creating a clear, agreed-upon vision for the teaching and learning of mathematics that defines what you are doing and shapes your actions. The vision identifies what the team hopes the school's math program will accomplish and will guide the school in the creation of a four-year plan for the teaching of mathematics. The plan is detailed, concretely showing how the different outcomes are being developed over four years, from grade to grade, and includes individual units, lessons, activities, performance tasks, and projects. Questions that teams of teachers can think about as they develop this plan are provided below.

- How will your school develop an inquiry-based approach to teaching that will make the outcomes presented in this document possible? What experiences will students have in year one? Two? Three? Four? For example, what experiences will students have with open-ended problems/tasks in year one? Two? Three? Four? How will the tasks change? How will expectations for students change?
- How will student mathematical proficiency be developed over four years? What will student conceptual understanding look like after year one? Two? Three? Four? What will student procedural fluency look like after year one? Two? Three? Four?
- How will student development as mathematical problem solvers develop over four years? What will that development look like in year one? Two? Three? Four?
- How will student ability to explain, justify, and prove develop over four years? What will that look like in year one? Two? Three? Four?
- How will students develop as reflective learners over four years? What will that look like in year one? Two? Three? Four?
- How will students develop as mathematical thinkers over four years? What will that look like in year one? Two? Three? Four?
- How will students' beliefs, attitudes, and perceptions change over four years? What types of experiences will students have over the four years to make for that change? What will that look like in year one? Two? Three? Four?

References

Boaler, J. (1997). *Experiencing school mathematics.* Buckingham, UK: Open University Press.

Borasi, R. (1992). *Learning mathematics through inquiry.* Portsmouth, NH: Heinemann.

Burns, M., and Humpreys, C. (1990). *A collection of math lessons: From grade 6 through 8.* Sausalito, CA: Math Solutions Publications.

Common Core State Standards Initiative. (2011). *Common Core State Standards for Mathematics.* [Electronic version]. Retrieved May 16, 2011 from http://www.corestandards.org/.

Conley, D. T. (2007). *Toward a comprehensive conception of college readiness.* Eugene, OR: Educational Policy Improvement Center.

Driscoll, M. (1999). *Fostering algebraic thinking.* Portsmouth, NH: Heinemann.

Driscoll, M. (2007). *Fostering geometric thinking.* Portsmouth, NH: Heinemann.

Fendel, D., Resek, D., Alper, L., and Fraser, S. (1999). *Interactive mathematics program.* Emeryville, CA: Key Curriculum Press.

Hersh R. (1997). *What is mathematics really?* Oxford: Oxford University Press.

Hiebert, J., Carpenter, T., Fennema, E., Fuson, K., Wearne, D., Murray, H., Olivier, A., and Human, P. (1997). *Making sense: Teaching and learning mathematics with understanding.* Portsmouth, NH: Heinemann.

Katz, J. (2009). Teacher and student perceptions of conventional and inquiry-based mathematics instruction. (Dissertation)

Koehler, M., and Grouws, D. A. (1992). "Mathematics teaching practices and their effects." In D. A. Grouws, ed., *Handbook of research on mathematics teaching and learning*, 115–26. New York: Macmillan.

Lampert, M. (1990). "When the problem is not the question and the solution is not the answer: Mathematical knowing and teaching." *American Education Research Journal* 27 (1): 29–63.

Lockhart, P. (2012). *Measurement.* Cambridge, MA: Harvard University Press.

McDonald, J., Mohr, N., Dichter, A., and McDonald, E. (2003). *The Power of Protocols.* New York: Teachers College Press.

National Council of Teachers of Mathematics. (2000). *Principles and standards for school mathematics* (J. Carpenter, S. Gregg, and W. Martin, eds.). Reston, VA: Author.

National Research Council. (1996). *National science educational standards.* Washington, DC: National Academy Press.

National Research Council. (2001). *Adding it up: Helping children learn mathematics* (J. Kilpatrick, J. Swafford, and B. Findell, eds.). Mathematics Learning Study Committee, Center of Education, Division of Behavioral and Social Sciences and Education. Washington, DC: National Academy Press.

Nicol, C., and Crespo, S. (2005). "Exploring mathematics in imaginative places: Rethinking what counts as meaningful contexts for learning mathematics." *School Science and Mathematics* 105 (5): 240–51.

Philipp, R. (2007). Mathematics teachers' beliefs and affect. In F. A. Lester, ed., *Second handbook of research on mathematics teaching and learning*, 257–315. Charlotte, NC: Information Age Publishing.

Polya, G. (1945). *How to solve it.* Princeton, NJ: Princeton University Press.

Senge, P. et al. (1994) The *fifth discipline fieldbook: Strategies and tools for building a learning organization.* New York: Crown.

Senk, S. L., and Thompson, D. R. (2003). "School mathematics curricula: Recommendations and issues." In S. L. Senk ane D. R. Thompson, eds., *Standards-based school curricula: What are they? What do students learn?*, 3–27. Mahwah, NJ: Lawrence Erlbaum Associates.

Stinson, D. W. (2004). "Mathematics as "gate-keeper"(?): Three theoretical perspectives that aim toward empowering all children with a key to the gate." *The Mathematics Educator* 14 (1): 8–18.

Suchman, J. R. (1968). *Inquiry development program in earth science.* Chicago: Science Research Associates.

Wells, G. (1999). *Dialogic inquiry: Towards a sociocultural practice and theory of education.* New York: Cambridge University Press.

Index

About the Author

For more than three decades **Jonathan D. Katz** has been engaged in looking at and appreciating mathematics for its wonder, beauty and power. He taught mathematics in New York City public schools for 23 years to students from grades 6 to 12. For the past 10 years he has worked with teachers across the country as a mathematics coach to support the development of mathematical thinking and understanding in their students.

He completed his doctoral studies at Teachers College Columbia University where his focus was on teacher and student perceptions of conventional and inquiry-based instruction.